# It *is* Well

# It *is* Well

## Finding Joy in the Middle of My Mess

### TABITHA SNEEDEN

XULON PRESS

Xulon Press Elite
2301 Lucien Way #415
Maitland, FL 32751
407.339.4217
www.xulonpress.com

Unless otherwise indicated, Scripture quotations taken from the Holy Bible, New International Version (NIV). Copyright © 1973, 1978, 1984, 2011 by Biblica, Inc.™. Used by permission. All rights reserved.

Printed in the United States of America.
Edited by Xulon Press.

ISBN-13: 9781545621196

# Introduction

The inspiration for this book is the result of many years of writing both poems and stories about my life. As a child, I wrote poems and gave them as gifts to my parents for holidays or birthdays. Later on, I wrote to express different stages of life I was going through. I've written during both happy and dark times, reflecting on God as He revealed Himself in all of these various situations—everything from motherhood, military family life, church leadership, to my nursing career provided ample opportunity to see our very faithful God at work. Writing also provides a therapeutic way of healing through loss and helping me to see that there is always a bigger, better plan taking place. The biggest thing I've learned is that God cares about every little detail of our lives. When we learn to quiet ourselves, He speaks most clearly and is capable to provide for even our most trivial need.

I'd like to thank my parents, Rod and Elaine Marlow, for always being a great example and pointing me to Christ. Even when we lived in Alaska and you had to fly to see the grandchildren, you were there for us. I can't imagine surviving Bryan's deployments without being able to call you on the phone (pretty much daily) and for all the support and advice you gave to us. I'd also like to thank the ladies of Thrive Community Church in Grand Forks, North Dakota, for the opportunity to stretch myself and my faith through leadership. I deeply apologize for not keeping in touch since we moved back to Illinois. I learned the difficult lesson that moving home is not always the easy move that we presume it will be. The next chapter of our lives would be challenging, and finding a church like Thrive has been nearly impossible. There's a piece of this book specifically written for the ladies of Thrive, which I hope will convey the deep impact that you've made in our lives and how much our family misses all of you.

My hope and prayer is that you will be blessed beyond measure as you read this book. Each chapter stands alone and can be read in any order you like. My ultimate goal is to glorify our God for the incredible, awesome, loving, enduring, and merciful God that He is.

Perhaps you will begin to notice tiny blessings in your own life each day, and together we will worship our God—a God who cares about the details.

In Christian love,

Tabitha

# Dedication

This book is dedicated to my wonderful husband, Bryan, without whom I simply cannot function. I'm forever grateful that God put the two of us together. Thanks for putting up with me during times when life was complicated. Our marriage is the best gift ever.

The book is also dedicated to my mother. Without you, I wouldn't even be here to be inspired and to share this message. You have always been my biggest cheerleader, and I love you endlessly.

# Acknowledgments

I'd like to specifically acknowledge some individuals for their continued support during this process: My husband has been extremely instrumental in providing support and feedback. There were times that the writing was flowing well, and he understood that I needed time to get it all together. I know the book of our life together has many more chapters. I'm sure it will inspire more writing. I know you'll be there for all of it, and I love you to the moon and back. You are truly my best friend and a blessing straight from God.

My mom and my mother-in-law were important during this writing process. Each of them shared journals, which added to the depth of what I was writing. Sharon shared the journal of how Bryan's dad was saved from leukemia and how he came back to Christ during that terrible illness. Mom shared a journal that her mother had written, in which she shared her childhood stories. I'm so grateful that both of you shared because I came to a better understanding of what took place in each of their lives (my Grandma's and Butch's), and it was incredibly helpful while I was writing.

Mom and Dad: Thank you for always showing me Christ. I know life doesn't always go the way you plan, but there's a lesson to be learned in every circumstance. Thank you for loving me, even when I was unlovable.

Additionally, I'd like to thank Paul G. Sir—you know who you are—and during the short time that we had to visit and talk about God, you shared some incredible wisdom. Thanks for your advice to be more descriptive and ask God to help me expand my writings.

Finally, I'd like to thank Thrive Community Church in Grand Forks, North Dakota: Thank you for supporting our family during our time with you. Also, thank you for utilizing us in leadership and for helping us to mature in our faith. The opportunities you provided to serve will remain forever in our hearts. The unique mission of your church fulfils such a need in the community. I honestly wish there was a clone of Thrive near every single military installation in America. Military families need the kind of support that you continue to provide. The good news of Christ is a message that will never be silenced. Keep doing what you're doing. Keep growing. We love you and thank God for you.

# Pen Pals

To begin, allow me to describe my life. I was born in the early '70s, and my Dad was the pastor of a small, independent Christian church in Illinois. Throughout my childhood, I would live in Illinois, Tennessee (where my brother was born), Mississippi, and Kentucky. During my second-grade year, our family moved back to Illinois. I grew up loving church and loving God. We were in attendance every service unless we ran a temperature or had some awful illness. Church was our life. My mom stayed home with us until my brother entered school, and my dad worked several jobs to make ends meet. I remember he drove a school bus and also worked as a locksmith during my grade school years. When I was ten, my dad went back to school to attain a degree in mortuary science. This would allow him to change vocations and work as a licensed funeral director.

I don't recall making a lot of friends at any one location. I might have had only a couple of close friends at any one place. Between the frequent moves and the stigma of my dad's career, not many kids wanted to know me. This was also the 1980s, so cell phones, the Internet, and e-mail didn't exist. Traditional letter writing was the only way for a girl to keep up with anyone. As you can imagine, I lost track of good friends over the years, and it would take twenty years and social media to reconnect me with them. By the time I finished college, I had moved eighteen to twenty times and attended 9 different schools Our family lived in several funeral homes (while my dad served for internships) until the last move I made with them during high school. During my sophomore year, we moved into the house in the town where I would finish high school and also attend college. It was more affordable for us if I commuted. At that time, I felt it would have killed me to move away from home.

During my middle school and high school years, I excelled at things that were artistic. I sang, acted in musicals and plays, and often had lead roles. My grades were average, and I found school challenging at every level. The only group I felt I fit into socially was with the choir kids or the theater kids. Everyone in my Sunday school class was secretly rebellious and only attended because their parents forced them. I attended church camps nearly every summer and always enjoyed the fellowship and environment. I'm told that even before I was old enough to be a camper, I was in attendance whether in utero or as a toddler. My dad was often the dean for a week of camp, and my mom would come along to function as camp nurse.

The very first job I held was as cashier at a local grocery store. I worked there for two years until entering college. I worked for about a year at DQ (the stickiest job ever) until I had completed my introductory nursing course and was qualified to be a nursing assistant at the local hospital. This was a great opportunity for me to get acquainted with the clinical environment and really see if I could handle nursing. I met some really wonderful nurses who knew I was in school and were willing to let me watch them place IVs or give injections. I was eager to see anything they were willing to show me, and it was actually during this time in my life that I met the woman who would become my mother-in-law.

It was the summer prior to my third year of college when a breakup with a boyfriend devastated me. I told the staffing office at the hospital that I was willing to work any shift they had available. My goal was to hide in the hospital all summer and avoid boys completely. I would immerse myself in nursing and give myself time to recover from having my heart broken. The week of my birthday (in June) I worked three overnights in a row with a great nurse named Sharon. Sharon was a Christian woman, a hard worker with a wicked sense of humor. By the end of the third shift, she was handing me an address with a picture of her son, whom she said was stationed at Andrews Air Force Base. She said she thought we'd get along great and asked if I would write to him. His name was Bryan, and he was a year older than me. I honestly didn't think we'd ever meet, but I liked writing letters, and Maryland was pretty far away from Illinois.

In October of 1992, Bryan came home for two weeks of leave prior to his one-year assignment in Korea. The entire first year of our relationship was spent writing letters to each other. I probably wrote him every day and spent enough on postage that I could have made a student loan payment. He returned to the States a year later, and on October 14, 1993, we were engaged. We were married on March 5, 1994, and three duty stations, two kids, and twenty-three years later, we are still together. God put us in the right places at the right times to carry out His perfect plan. Bryan's career in the Air Force has allowed us to live in Arkansas, Alaska, and North Dakota. As a nurse, I was able to work in all of these places in the civilian setting, while we raised our two wonderful children. We've seen the world and made friends for life at each location. As expected, life is full of drama, pain, and often disappointment. Retrospectively, I see the carefully orchestrated plan God has carried out, though I don't understand it all. My role is to simply trust and obey. It may take my entire life to work out what it means to totally live by faith. It takes practice to give God every burden, every stress, and every need every day of your life and to trust that He's got a plan to work it all out. But, I'm a child of God in need of grace.

This is who I am.

# Bloom Where You're Planted

As a military wife, I've lived a lot of places and seen a lot of things. I've moved our family from base to base, survived all kinds of climates, unusual neighborhood situations, and even functioned as a single parent for months at a time. My civilian friends could never fathom how our family functioned. It seems that only fellow military understand or appreciate what the life involves. This has been consistently true everywhere we've lived. When you encounter other military members, regardless of branch, there is a unique comradery you don't find with any other demographic. Life in service of your country is very special and should be valued. It's also an honor to take care of those who have served because it makes us all brothers and binds us in a way which nothing else can.

Our very first base as a married couple was Little Rock Air Force Base. The hot and humid climate was always a challenge. Bryan was sent to Italy for three months and missed our first wedding anniversary. After Laina was born, they sent him to Louisiana for survival training for a month. My mother had to come back down from Illinois to stay with me because I was having postnatal complications. Bryan had several deployments to the Middle East during our six years stationed there. There were plenty of times he would leave on deployment and not be able to call me for over a week. I was a nervous wreck, waiting for that first call. He wouldn't be able to tell me exactly where he was or the status of leaving to return home. As a wife, I wanted to know as much as I could, but he wasn't allowed to tell me finite details of his travel on the phone. I worked full-time and managed two little ones while he was gone. Thanks to my church, I had some help. We were about seven hours from our parents, so it was possible to drive home and visit several times a year, or they'd each come to see us and the kids. Raising little ones and working kept me plenty busy.

Our second base was Eielson Air Force Base in Alaska. We drove up there in February of 2000 with a three-year-old and a four-month-old. Brandon was cutting teeth the entire trip, so you can imagine what fun we all had. Once we arrived and got our housing,

Bryan had orders for the Middle East already waiting at his shop. Our tour in Alaska was for four years, and Bryan would spend two of four summers in the desert. This time, we were far away from family, and they had to fly to visit. Both sets of parents flew up once during that four-year tour. Luckily, long distance was still cheap because I called my mother every day that Bryan was deployed. Seasonal depression was an unfortunate fact during this tour. I found myself needing antidepressants, like so many other people. Then, the insomnia during the never-ending days of summer also posed a problem. Eventually, you figure it out, and life feels normal again. I worked full-time at a clinic in downtown Fairbanks, and this helped to give me purpose and make ends meet. During those four years, the kids grew like weeds. I started getting into photography while we were stationed there as a way to preserve the beautiful wildflowers we saw on our adventures. I had bought a book on Alaskan wildflowers and found that many of them were poisonous if consumed. Collecting physical specimens to press into a book was not an option—small kids seem to put everything in their mouths. Instead, I photographed them, which became a hobby of mine.

The tragedy of 9/11 happened while we were stationed in Alaska. I remember that day so clearly. I had just dropped of the kids at daycare and was getting back into my car to head to work. One of the neighbors from our street came running out of her house, frantic about everyone turning on the news. I went back into the house to watch footage of the twin towers being hit by a plane and then collapsing. It was frightful and scary. The base went on high alert, and security was tight. For the rest of our time stationed there, our vehicle would be searched both entering and leaving the base. For months, this incident was discussed on every form of media possible, and you couldn't escape hearing about it. Alaskans were fearful that the oil pipeline would be bombed, destroying the entire state. Thankfully, that never happened. Terrorists accomplished what they set out to do, which was to instill fear. Many lives were lost that day, and the event lives in the heart of every American. I can't imagine facing this fear without the hope of a living God in my life. Without this hope, I think it would have been hard to function.

Our third base was at Grand Forks Air Force Base in North Dakota. We arrived in February of 2004 and were stationed there for the last seven years of Bryan's career. North Dakota is famous for blizzards and wind. We saw temperatures far colder than during our tour in Alaska! Hoping to live someplace further south, we had put in for bases in other climates, but God intended for us to be there. I prayed to find some kind of hobby to call my own. I had to have something to do that was mine alone and would make me less miserable in a place so boring and flat. We enjoyed exploring state parks as a family, and there was one not too far from the base called Turtle River State Park. Going there was like an escape from the flatness, with its rolling hills and streams. There was a lot to see, and we went there often, either hiking or camping. I discovered lots of photo opportunities there, so I kept up the photography, and my pictures improved over time. North Dakota is famous for growing sunflowers, which I found really beautiful. There were fields of them everywhere. Photographing the fields became an interest of mine, and I enjoyed going for drives to find them. Bryan bought me a digital camera which replaced my 35 mm, and I'm still using that one today. I used it to record our life with busy kids in activities and things Bryan missed while he was on deployments. Recording our life in photographs was huge for me and a great creative outlet.

Deployments continued to be rough on the family. As kids grow and learn to understand the world, they can turn on the news and hear about world events, often becoming upset. The last deployment Bryan went on would take up most of eight months, including going to New Jersey for eight weeks of training. This was the toughest deployment by far, not because of the length, but because the kids were older. They worried about their dad and missed him. We often used Skype to stay connected, but sometimes seeing their dad made things worse. They knew what was going on in the world, and they feared for their dad's safety, along with missing him terribly. We took things one day at a time. Some days were okay, and other days were seemingly tragic, with lots of tears shed. There were a few times that we declared a pajama day, and we'd cuddle on the couch watching movies until we all felt better. We prayed nonstop for his safety and for God to help all of us get through one more day. I worked full-time at a hospital downtown and the kids were with a sitter after school. We'd been through this many times before, and I told myself we could do it one last time. Luckily, we had found Thrive Community Church and had more support than ever before. We had started attending the church a couple of years prior to this

27

deployment. I'm forever thankful for the mission of that church to support military families and for the ways we were involved in the ministry there. Because it was full of active-duty families, there was both sensitivity and an urgency to provide support to meet the needs we had. I was finally in a season where the kids weren't as physically dependent on me, and I had some free time to get involved in ministry. My involvement in helping to develop a basket ministry would give me an outlet I'd never had before. I prayed to God to use me as He saw fit, and I was blessed to find so much joy in ministry. It felt good to help meet the needs of others, to let God use me for a greater purpose, and it felt good to bloom where I was planted.

# Am I a Basket Case?

This particular piece was written while our family was stationed in North Dakota (sometime between 2004 and 2011). In it, I describe an outreach ministry that I helped to create. The church we attended at the time was specifically designed to meet the needs of the military family, as this community was unlike any other in its support for that particular demographic. Looking back presently, I'm so blessed that tiny seeds have grown into huge blessings for others. We left the church in May of 2011 upon Bryan's retirement from the military, and we moved back home to Illinois. What a bittersweet move that was. We were excited to move closer to family after so many years apart from them, but our time with Thrive Community Church opened our hearts to ministry in serving others.

When it comes to community outreach, the opportunities are endless. Depending on your location and the cultures in your area, a little creativity can go a long way. I experienced a unique form of outreach that blossomed into a wonderful blessing for many. Not only were the recipients blessed, but what returned to me was ten-fold. I never knew God could use an idea I had for the Kingdom, and I'm learning daily how He uses each one of us.

To preface an explanation of the basket ministry, I should explain that I am a military spouse. My husband had been in the Air Force for nearly twenty years, and this was our third base together as a family. In May of 2006, my husband deployed to Iraq for several months. My children (then ten and seven) had been through this before; however, this deployment was more stressful than usual. We were struggling with finding a church to meet our needs as a military family. Our nearest relatives were seventeen hours away, so it was imperative that we develop relationships with a church that could help us in times like deployment. With no inde-pendent Christian churches for at least fifty miles, we had chosen a Nazarene church to attend. The doctrine was similar, but since we are military (and essentially transient); it was difficult to make lasting friendships with the people there. When my husband left for this deployment, I instantly felt orphaned (spiritually orphaned, to be exact). My phone never rang to see if there was anything I needed. I received no e-mails from anyone from the church. It was well-known that the kids and I would be alone for four months, yet there was no outreach to us. As a pastor's kid, this was hurtful to me. I felt empty and as if I didn't belong.

This need to belong left me searching for a new church. Even without my husband in the country, I owed it to myself and to the children to be spiritually fed. For the length of the deployment, I would be their only parent. I needed the support of other Christians to make it through this trying time apart from Bryan, and I needed to be a part of something bigger than me. I needed to be filled, so Christ could continue to use me, and at that moment I was hurting, empty, and overwhelmed.

The new church welcomed us with open arms. They met at the local YMCA and made use of a large gym and the children's facilities in the building. They advertised that they were specifically reaching out to military families and to students of the local university. Only in existence for a few months, they already seemed to have a thriving children's ministry, and my kids dove immediately into that program. I remember the woman at the registration table and her smiling face. She offered my kids a name tag and introduced herself as "Miss Becky." There was warmth in her eyes that I can't explain, other than just knowing she seemed to understand me. I found out later that her husband was a pilot for the Air Force, and she knew all too well the stresses of being alone with two children. That very week I received a card in the mail from Becky in which she said how much she had enjoyed meeting us and having the kids in Children's church. She added in the card that if there was anything we needed to please contact her, and someone would assist me. I cried when I read that card! It meant so much that someone understood and reached out. To this day, Becky is one of my dearest friends, and we served God together side-by-side during our time at Thrive Community Church.

Becky, as I found, was also in charge of the women's ministry. I immediately got involved in this and felt led to be used by God to reach others. The idea for the basket ministry came directly from Becky's card to me. If I could help other military wives feel that a church was interested in their lives and concerned for their well-being, they could find a church home. They could create a network of reliable friends and make this time of separation a bit easier. I wanted other military wives to find what I had found. This new church was full of opportunities to serve and to grow in our relationship with God. After three Sundays, I was ready to give back. My cup was full, and I was ready.

Becky gave me the go-ahead to make a few baskets. At first, I was purchasing items myself, finding things on clearance or at thrift stores. Later, the women from our Bible study group donated things like candles, chocolates, small stuffed animals for children, or other items. On average, our baskets usually contained a mug, coffees or teas, chocolates, bath salts, lotions, candles, or anything that could help a stressed wife and mother to relax. For the children, we included a small stuffed animal, and there was always a card from the group, listing phone numbers of our ladies in leadership. They could contact any one of us if there was a need. These baskets were distributed to any woman we knew to be alone because of military deployment. Some of these women were currently attending our church, and others had no church affiliation. Our goal was to encourage every woman whose name we received and to provide support.

James 1:27 (NIV) calls us to "look after the orphans and widows." And in 2:16–17, we are further encouraged to take action in providing for the physical needs of the less fortunate. What better time is there to reach a scared family than when a husband is deployed to war? A majority of the women to participate in our ministry had active duty husbands and each of us had experienced the stresses of war and separation. By providing for the physical, emotional, and spiritual needs of our fellow military, we demonstrated the compassionate and unconditional love of Christ. Additionally, the body of Christ grew and anxieties were greatly reduced with a "peace that transcends all understanding" (Philippians 4:7, NIV).

The result of this project was phenomenal to say the least. Sixteen months into this project, our group delivered twenty baskets to military families. About half of these were to active churchgoers and strengthened friendships. The other half were delivered to women who were without a church family and many at least made a visit to our church. Regardless of affiliation, most recipients commented that they felt so blessed to know that someone was praying for them and for their deployed spouse. They knew that, when they called the contact numbers on the card, they were not inconveniencing anyone (this was an important factor). The children each had something small but tangible that let them know we were thinking of them, and through this outreach, hearts were touched for Christ. A close friend of mine commented to me that even her sixth-grade son clung to his stuffed animal at night. Younger children, of course, carried theirs everywhere they went. Providing comfort and encouragement was the ultimate goal.

The success we had with military baskets prompted us to include the college-aged population in a basket outreach. Right before final exams in December, we assembled fifty baskets from the local dollar store. We put out an e-mail to the congregation and were able to fill all of these baskets with items for finals week. They included microwave popcorn, soda, bottled water, candies, gum, and granola bars. In addition, we included a handwritten card for each basket, expressing encouragement. Each card stated that the recipient would be prayed for during final exams and wished them great success. We had twenty students in attendance to receive these baskets, and each took additional ones for roommates or classmates. Some of these resulted in greater attendance from the college crowd and a greater willingness for them to check out our Sunday service.

Our small but growing church blossomed into something wonderful! The opportunities to serve Christ through community outreach were endless. More importantly, our relationship with the local university and Air Force base gave us the unique opportunity to reach out to more distinct groups: spouses and children of deployed soldiers and college students away from home. When people are lonely and hurting, their hearts are often open to the idea of a loving God who cares for them. By being His hands and His feet, the women in our church experienced the joy of giving and sharing Christ. There also came a point at which I chose to pass the basket ministry to another member of our group. This left me more time to be the leader of the women's ministry. My good friend, Becky, continues to function as children's minister and secretary for our church, and she is an incredible leader. It's a pleasure to serve God alongside such talented and generous women. The joy you receive when you give of yourself cannot be measured. And, when you give of yourself, you give the very best.

# Blessings

Throughout our lives, our closeness with God seems to be on a continuum. During certain times in our lives, we may feel that we are in the middle of God's perfect will. Other times, maybe because of our hectic schedules or struggles, we can drift. Thankfully, there is always that invitation to return to that closeness where you are relying on God daily through His word, prayer, and fellowship.

Throughout my husband's military career we lived in several states, and it was often difficult to find a church home. The ministry system you find on the military bases are not allowed to do much more than present the fluffy message that God loves you. In speaking with an Air Force chaplain, I discovered that what they present to the military community is often dictated by the higher-ranking officers. They are not allowed to present a message of conviction, but rather the simple message of God's love. They present a warm, fuzzy, sugar-coated version of Christianity. They can ask you about what you believe and "How's that working for you?" but they are not allowed to challenge or convict through their message. Traditional civilian churches don't have these boundaries, so we really strived to find an off-base Christian church to meet our spiritual needs. It's also difficult to find a civilian church to meet our needs as a military family.

We were lucky enough to find a church in North Dakota, while we were stationed there, which was designed specifically to meet the needs of the military family and the college community. Both of these demographics are unique in that there is this nonstop revolving door of people in and out. Most duty assignments are minimum two years, and depending on the mission of the base or squadron, deployments can be frequent. The goal of Thrive Community Church seemed to be creation of a feeling of closeness with Christian believers, regardless of the ever-changing faces. This type of church is dramatically different. We had more goodbye parties than anything else, but these presented constant opportunity to show the love of God in such a unique way.

I had the rare opportunity to help start up a ministry for women and families that would forever change me. We specifically served the spouses and children of active duty members. Deployments of soldiers overseas are stressful for families, and families either rely on their neighbors on base or the squadron they are members of. My personal goal was to always be independent while my husband was gone and to not need help of any kind. I always managed my own yard care, child care, and auto issues and preferred to rely on my church family before contacting the squadron. Another chapter in this book directly discusses the basket ministry we started up to demonstrate God's love to the active duty military families. This program blessed me as much as the families we served.

Men's ministry was very active, and Bryan found his place alongside men with common interests. These guys hunted, fished, golfed, and did all sorts of activities together. Bible study and prayer were part of every activity, and strong friendships were created. The kids also enjoyed the youth programming, attending church camp one summer and growing in their faith under the tutelage of couples we'd known for years as devoted Christians. Our church had the largest baptistery in town (the YMCA pool is pretty large), and both of our kids were baptized as believers during our time with Thrive Community Church. Vacation Bible school was also a hit, as we came together to provide this outreach to our community. Everyone helped with snacks, activities, and skits and gave their all as we showed Christ to kids of all ages. Our time with Thrive helped to prepare us for the next chapter of our lives, though it has been difficult to find a church home after retirement from the military. We rely on the faith we developed to get us through each new chapter and know God has more in store for our family as we watch our children reach adulthood.

The friendships that we grew there have changed us in ways I can't describe. I do remember one particular summer when Bryan was deployed. I continued my ministry as usual and had no intention of backing off on my commitments to the church community. However, the kids were older, and I was still working full-time as a nurse downtown. A couple we knew well, who hadn't been married very long, stepped up in a surprising way to support our family. I received a card that said the couple was not only covering the cost of art camp for our daughter, but were providing transportation and were also going to entertain our son while I worked. This was a complete surprise and came out of the blue. What a blessing to us! Laina enjoyed her art/music camp, and Brandon got to go golfing several times. This got us through what could have been a very rough summer with Bryan deployed.

It's amazing to me how God works out even the tiniest detail. Even now, though we no longer live in North Dakota, the mission is clear. When we make ourselves available to be used for the purpose of blessing others and bringing them to Christ, the return on the investment is profound. I continue to pray that our family will be used by God so that His love is continually evident to everyone around us. Our lives are the biggest and best testimony there is to the goodness of God.

# Surprise Attack

During our time at Thrive Community church, our family grew in our faith. Our involvement in activities and service resulted in a closer walk with God and more joy than we had ever experienced. One thing I have found to be consistently true, however, is that the closer you get to God, the more Satan attacks. I'm amazed at his sheer craftiness. He'll use any and all means to prevent you from fellowship with other believers or to upset the balance in your life. It's all smoke and mirrors and pure distraction. If he can take your eyes of the mission for one moment, perhaps he can dismantle God's Kingdom work. He tries very hard, but if you can catch him in the act and call him on the carpet, he'll leave you alone.

I recall one specific attack that happened, in which he used my husband to derail God's mission. It was a Tuesday night, and I was waiting for Bryan to come home from work. We were going to grill something outside to go with the other things I was fixing for supper. The plan for the evening was that after supper, I would leave to attend our weekly ladies' book club, and he was going to watch the kids. The homework was done already, and we just needed to get the grill started. From the moment Bryan walked in, something was wrong. He was in a foul mood and very quickly said something to me that hurt my feelings. He walked out the patio door, and at that moment, I was so upset. I started to cry because of what he said, and in my head I began trying to figure out what I could have possibly done to promote that type of response from him. To this day, I don't remember exactly what he said that immediately upset me.

Realizing what had just happened, I called Laina into the kitchen, and we began to pray. I denounced Satan and said he could not have my family today or any other day. I demanded that he leave immediately! "In the name of Jesus, I demand that you leave now." I practically shouted this over and over and then after a couple of minutes, things felt calmer. I dried my eyes and thanked Laina for praying with me and continued setting the table for supper. A few minutes later, Bryan emerged from outside, and he was completely different. Seriously. It was as if that hurtful conversation had never even happened because his tone and attitude were completely changed in the ten minutes he'd been outside. He came in acting sweet and loving, as usual, which is how he usually acts toward me and the kids. The whole incident was strange, but I know in my heart I had just thwarted a direct attack from Satan.

Had I not recognized the attack for what it was, things would have gone much differently. If I had become too upset, I might have decided not to attend my group meeting and would have texted one of my friends to say I wasn't feeling well enough to go. Had I missed that meeting, I would have missed the message, the fellowship and the chance to support someone in the name of Jesus. Satan would have loved to have prevented me from going, and he definitely gave it his best shot. He strikes more often when we are on fire for God and when our mission is clear. Other times, Satan uses the sin in our lives to make us ineffective. He gets inside our heads and whispers that we will never be good enough. He tries to convince us that we've fallen too far to be of any use. He stifles the testimony we have to share and shuts us up when we should be sharing our story. That negative self-talk is terribly damaging. If we start to believe

Satan's lies, Kingdom growth is stunted. We cannot let him win. We have to arm ourselves and prepare for battle with him. We have to learn to recognize his attacks and call him out.

The Bible clearly states that our battle is not with flesh and blood but with dark and evil spiritual forces. Don't let that scare you. The book of Revelation describes that final battle in which God will fight against Satan and tells us that God wins. We have this assurance that good will triumph over evil and Satan will be defeated once and for all. I find great comfort in knowing that I'm on the winning side of this war, and you should, too. As for family drama; well, sometimes it's drama, and sometimes it's not. Pray for discernment to know the difference between daily squabbles and a blatant attack from the evil one. Keep talking, praying, and serving as a family. Kick Satan out of your head and out of your home and declare him defeated in the name of Jesus. Arm yourself with scripture and pray daily so that he doesn't stand a chance.

# Nailed it

My entire life, I have always envied anyone who could grow long, beautiful nails. Most of the women in my family have this ability, but I do not. I've tried every strengthener, hardener, and supplement with no improvement. A few times in my life, I've had artificial nails put on in the salon, but they never last long. As a nurse, it's too difficult to maintain them with all the handwashing and getting in and out of gloves all day. My cleaning routine at home is a setup for complete disaster, so I'm really not into fake nails. I hoped prenatal supplements during my pregnancies would help my nails grow out. My hair grew incredibly during that time, but the nails continued to split, crack, and peel.

The only thing that ever helped my nails to grow out was paying for the expensive chip-free manicure at the salon. It doesn't involve an artificial nail being placed, so the difference between this modality and anything else is that it's my natural nail underneath with an incredibly strong top coat on top. This coating allows me to grow out my nails naturally while protecting them from everything I do that would destroy them. Without this fortifying layer on top, I'm back where I began with nails that are weak and thin.

A scripture comes to mind about the kind of fortification God can provide. We need to arm ourselves to protect against the world and its caustic environment. Just as household chemicals or frequent handwashing can destroy my nice manicure, facing Satan without support can be equally as devastating. We are constantly bombarded by the world and all it has to offer. Christians must:

Put on the full armor of God, so that when the day of evil comes, you may be able to stand your ground, and after you have done everything, to stand. Stand firm then, with the belt of truth buckled around your waist, with the breastplate of righteousness in place, and with your feet fitted with the readiness that comes from the gospel of peace. In addition to all this, take up the shield of faith, with which you can extinguish all the flaming arrows of the evil one. Take the helmet of salvation and the sword of the Spirit, which is the word of God. (Ephesians 6:13–17)

This is serious stuff.

Applying this armor happens through reading of God's word and prayer. Make time daily to let God speak to you and show you how to maintain this level of fortification. With the right kind of support, your faith will grow unhindered.

# Tea Time

T ea has a long history, going back for centuries. And, while it isn't mentioned in the Bible, tea trade routes opened up new frontiers for evangelism. You can find a ton of information about its origins and how tea is utilized in both nonreligious and religious practices all over the world. There's much to be learned about etiquette, tea types, preparation methods, and serving techniques. The common denominator, regardless of tea type, is the use of boiling hot water to brew it.

I confess that before I was educated, I had taken shortcuts to brew my tea. I had even microwaved it. But now that I know more, I refuse to take shortcuts or compromise for the sake of quality and benefit. It blew my mind that something as simple as the water temperature could make or break my tea time. It's true. It's also true in the Christian life, and there is a distinct parallel between the two.

In Revelation 3:15–16, God tells the church at Laodicea, through the apostle John, that He wishes they "were either hot or cold." Lukewarm doesn't work for tea, and it doesn't work with God. We've got to be on fire (boiling hot) and eager to get into His word and use it in our lives. When you put boiling water and tea leaves together, you brew a dark and flavorful, antioxidant-rich beverage. It's comforting and good for you and has healthful benefits. Similarly, when we get on fire for God and add Him to our lives, we get a rich, meaningful, everlasting relationship with Him that has everlasting benefits.

I encourage you to be on fire, if you aren't already. You'll brew up an incredible life in Christ.

# Walking on the Streets of "Bling"

This chapter contains a devotion I wrote during the time I served in leadership for the women's ministry in North Dakota. My writing really exploded during this time, and I was constantly inspired by every day, ordinary experiences. When inspired, I'd write up my devotions and then share them as part of our weekly group meetings. Sometimes, we'd do a video study by a popular Christian author, and other times we'd do a book study. Regardless, the time of fellowship with these ladies was the highlight of my week.

Like many women, I began a new fitness kick as a New Year's resolution. I had a goal and in order to reach it, much effort was needed on my part. On an ordinary Saturday morning at the end of January at 0920, I set out on a mile walk and was thrilled because instead of going to the gym, I could walk outside. (Not that the gym is bad, but walking in circles does not thrill me, and fresh air is better). The temperature was forty degrees, and the skies were clear and sunny. It was unusual to have no wind, and since North Dakota is famous for wind, I was taking advantage of the moment. So, I grabbed my iPod, shades, and outerwear and headed out. The entire walk was amazing, and the wind never kicked up once.

Midway through my mile, a praise song came on that really hit home with me. Up until this point my arms were swaying at my sides, but when the message of the song registered with me, my hands went up and my eyes welled up with tears. Keep in mind that I grew up in a church where a gal's hands never left her lap, so it took a lot for me to be this inspired. The message of the song was about how everything in our lives needs to bring praise to God. What an incredible message! "This is what I long for," I thought to myself. And, with my eyes partly closed, I continued walking and praising—not caring if cars passed me and people thought I was nuts.

The song ended, and when I fully opened my eyes again, I took notice of how sparkly the path was before me. Snow-moving equipment had indeed been through and only a sheer layer of snow remained on the walkway. Thanks to the bright sunshine, every inch of concrete simply glittered! (I'm sure my preteen daughter would say it had "bling"). It was breathtaking, and I was completely enthralled in such a simple thing. Suddenly, a thought entered my mind, "If you think this is great, just wait until you see Heaven." (Okay, now *this* is the part where I knew God was talking, and it was my job just to listen.) My entire life I had heard Christian speakers talk about hearing God and how God spoke through situations. I admit that growing up as a pastor's kid, I had always *hoped* to hear the voice of God somehow but had never experienced it. I'd never had any great stories of my own until this past year. For me, He seems to speak in a breeze or in the falling leaves. He never barges in loudly, but with the gentleness of a snowflake, His words fall upon me. When He speaks, it brings this incredible, quiet joy that builds until I have no choice but to share it with my closest friends.

Revelation, chapter 21, vividly describes the heaven God is preparing for us. Even with my college-educated mind, there are names of precious stones that I cannot pronounce, much less imagine. Add to this, the gates made of pearl and the streets of gold, and you have something that would put your jaw on the floor.

We cannot begin to fathom the "bling" God has in store for us in heaven. I was awed by this simple experience.

When I got home from my walk, I knew there were routine chores waiting for me. But, I was glad I chose to put my God time and physical maintenance before that. I think that we women often fail to take time for ourselves and time for God. We put everyone else's needs before our own, which is commendable. However, it's during those bits of time that you spend alone that God can speak to you. It came to mind also, that while the snow will linger for several more weeks, we all have spring cleaning in our hearts that cannot wait. So, start it now, before the thaw, and ask God for His guidance. And, don't forget to occasionally walk along the streets of "bling."

# Camouflage

The last time my husband put on his military uniform was May 5, 2011. Many people came together to celebrate what had been an outstanding military career of nearly twenty-two years. It was a simple ceremony, but it held great meaning for our family. I've been told that some soldiers plan much more elaborate events by renting out the enlisted club or a hall for this event. Bryan's simply took place in the shop where he worked every day. Some pass out tokens to commemorate the occasion and have music and flowery presentations. Since I'd never attended a retirement ceremony prior to this, I had nothing to compare it to. In my opinion, I would have loved to honor Bryan with something bigger and better, but he's not that kind of guy. He keeps things simple and gets things done. Sometimes, that's the best way.

At his request, the event was by invitation only. We picked up the kids from school, so they could be present to honor their dad's years of military service. The ceremony was brief but incredibly special to us. Certificates of appreciation were presented to Bryan and to me as a supportive spouse. Unknown to me, much would be said of the kids and me as aides to Bryan's unselfish service. I was so honored and never saw it coming when the squadron commander gave a speech and then Bryan gave one as well. I listened intently as he spoke such thoughtful words about his military career and retirement. It was a difficult speech to make, and I don't know how I managed to keep my composure while he shared about how difficult it was to leave for his last deployment. It was the longest trip he'd made away from us, and it was the worst thing of all to break the news to our young son. Brandon was ten when he and Bryan went on a hunting trip with some local friends. It was during their time away that he told him he had to leave again. This news didn't go over well, as you can imagine. It must have broken his heart to tell Brandon because it broke all of ours to hear the story retold.

After that, I received flowers and appreciation for being "the rock" that kept the family going while Bryan was deployed. I was honored and touched to be mentioned but assumed today was all about my husband. It was wonderful to hear such lovely words. He was clear that the mission could not be successful without a great team at home. He emphasized the importance of a great spouse and then also the importance of education. He urged young airmen to take advantage of the opportunity to finish college and that they shouldn't procrastinate. Ah, the wisdom of experience!

This was one of the proudest moments of my adult life. It feels good to have played a huge role in my husband's success. In the Bible, God gave Adam a wife to be a helpmeet. You can read all about that in the book of Genesis, and then in the New Testament, Christ talks a great deal about love and respect between a husband and his wife. Ephesians 5:22–33 explains it in this way:

Wives submit to your husbands as to the Lord. For the husband is the head of the wife as Christ is the head of the church, his body of which he is the Savior. Now as the church submits to Christ, so also wives should submit to their husbands in everything. Husbands, love your wives, just as Christ loved the church and gave himself up for her to make her holy, cleansing her by the washing with water through the word, and to present her to himself as a radiant church, without stain or wrinkle or any other blemish, but holy and blameless. In this same way, husbands ought to love their wives as their own bodies. He who loves his wife loves himself. After all, no one ever hated his own body, but he feeds and cares for it, just as Christ does the church—for we are members of his body. For this reason a man will leave his father and mother and be united to his wife, and the two will become one flesh. This is a profound mystery—but I am talking about Christ and the church. However, each one of you also must love his wife as he loves himself, and the wife must respect her husband.

We've all heard messages in church, which cover this topic, and I want to remind you that this scripture doesn't mean that either my husband or I are slaves to one another or that either of us is unrelentingly bossy and hard to deal with. When your life is anchored in

Christ, loving each other and showing respect is part of that natural process. Whether Bryan was stationed back home or was sent far away, we functioned as a team the very best that we could, and I was convinced if we could get through his deployments, we could make it through anything.

It was difficult to see such a large chapter in our lives come to a close. All I knew was how to be a military spouse. Civilian life was ahead in the distance. I knew there's more to come for this family, and I couldn't wait to see what God had in store for us. The next chapter was unknown, but we trusted that "all things will work together for good for those who love God and are called according to His purpose" (Romans 8:28).

# Write Like an Apostle

To preface this particular essay, I should explain that this is a letter I never sent. I should have sent it to the ladies of Thrive Community Church several years ago, but something stopped me. I made the huge mistake of assuming that Bryan's military retirement and moving back to Illinois was going to be the easiest move we made as a family. Instead, it was the most difficult move of all. Because the season that followed this move presented unforeseen challenges, I became afraid to reconnect with my North Dakota sisters in Christ. I was afraid they'd be either disappointed me, and in fact, I felt like a failure at that point in time. Still working to establish the kind of relationships we left behind, I continued my theory of "blooming where I'm planted." I greatly missed the friendship I shared with this special group of gals and the closeness. The support I experienced during our time together will never be forgotten. If I could go back in time to the year we moved, I would have shared the following devotion with them as part of a farewell and letter of thanks for all they continue to mean to me.

To the ladies of Thrive Community Church:

Greetings, my sisters! Tonight I feel like the apostle Paul, himself, is speaking through me. I remember memorizing long passages from Philippians in church camp as a child, never realizing how much Paul and I would have in common until today. His passion for the Lord inspires me, and as I've grown in my faith, I can certainly feel the emotion that exists in all he wrote during his ministry. Paul wrote what God inspired him to write. And, since the entire Bible is inspired by God, we cannot just believe it but use it as the standard for our lives. It provides us with inspiration we need to face our daily trials and shows how God uses imperfect people to carry out His perfect plan.

I find Paul extremely personable. Everywhere he went, he had a network of fellow believers, and he formed attachments. In reading the letters he wrote in the New Testament, you can feel how Paul was emotionally bonded to the early churches. He was fond of them and referred to them with endearments like "beloved" or "brethren," which give us a sense of family. He admonished them to love one another, to fellowship together, and to never lose heart. I've never had a church experience that measured up to Paul's "brotherly love" until Thrive Church. God blessed me with the unique opportunity to help start up a ministry for women in a very young church, and with His help, we are serving the Lord in an ever-increasing capacity. I have this huge desire to tell everyone to "consider it pure joy when they face trials," and that "to live is Christ and to die is gain" (James 1:2; Philippians 1:2)1. My head is so full of scriptures tonight! I love that I learned these passages years ago, and when the mood strikes, I can still recall them. It's times like these that they hold so much more meaning for me.

The thing I like the most about Paul is that he stayed connected to the churches by writing them letters. After he visited and helped establish them, he was inspired by God to keep encouraging them. He wrote of their strengths and of their deficits, detailing every struggle they faced. All of the churches were different, and each letter spoke of how much he missed them. Paul as devoted as a Christian can get, wanted everyone to find salvation and to stay on fire for God. I want to end this by saying that I hope to be very much like Paul (minus the jail time, of course). While my conversion wasn't dramatic or magical, Paul and I share the same muse. The same God, who inspired Paul, inspires me today. Sometimes I go months without writing, and then out of a special event comes an outpouring of words.

I can honestly say I understand the love of God. The depth, height, and extreme dimensions of His love for us are exactly how I feel about my Thrive family. Tonight as I'm about to sleep, I can wrap my head and heart around phrases like "I urge you, my brothers," as the sincerity in all your hugs and tears conveyed that same emotional intensity. Paul's wisdom into the heart of God is amazing to me. I've experienced agape love like never before in my relationships with all of you. So, as I move to my next location, I urge you, my sisters, to love and take care of each other, which you know is right, and to remember your first love, Jesus. Read the letters Paul wrote to the churches and with the same emotion that we've shared, come to a new understanding of what it means to be a follower of Christ. I thank you for letting me pour myself into your lives and while it upsets me to be leaving, I realize God pays attention to every detail. When He gives you friends, He gives you amazing ones.


In Christ,

Tabitha

# If the Dress Fits

S ome time ago, I was on social media and happened across a friend of mine who stated that after having five children, she could fit back into her wedding dress. I was rather inspired to get mine out of storage and see where I stood, myself. I hadn't seen this dress in twenty-three years, and it was in amazing shape. I remember distinctly that the fabric was Jessica McClintock brocade and that my mother had made it herself. *I loved this dress.* It was tea length with a drop waist and a full skirt. The style was slightly off-the-shoulder with a small capped sleeve. The day I wore it was historic for me, as it would be for any bride, and I couldn't wait to see if it still fit. Things were going well, right up until the zipper. I got it halfway up the back and then had to stop. Disappointed, I slipped it off and carefully put it back into my cedar chest. Despite how hard I battled to maintain a decent weight for my height and age, some parts of me are forever changed. I can't go back to being that rail-thin, twenty-one-year-old version of myself who didn't know what a stretch mark was. Still, it seems unfair not to be able to relive the most cherished and beautiful day of my life by fitting into that dress. I was understandably upset with myself.

I occurred to me that maybe I shouldn't be caught up in trying to attain this or be mad at myself that it didn't fit. After all, I'm not the same girl. Twenty-three years of marriage to my wonderful husband has brought a lot of change. Two grown children, several relocations, just as many jobs, tons of adventures, and endless memories have been mine to enjoy. The girl who wore that dress had never lived away from home. She didn't really know much of the world (and kind of liked it that way). She would work hard at the occupation that she went to school to train for, and over time, she would grow in her faith. Life experience would be the best teacher of all, and like anything else, marriage would require real work and dedication.

So much has changed in twenty-three years. My goals and aspi-

rations changed. I have matured and admit that in some ways (only

the good ones), I have become my mother. In fact, my husband

and I have both changed a lot over the course of our marriage.

I'm sure that right out of the gate; we had both compiled a list of things that annoyed us and things we wished to change about each other. I know I wasn't the best cook or the best housekeeper, and I wished he were more enthusiastic about church. The changes we needed to make did not happen overnight, and it wasn't up to us to force these changes in each other. The Holy Spirit, in His wisdom, brought about this change. It isn't our job. Our job was (and is) only to love each other and honor our spouse (and God) in how we conduct ourselves at all times.

First Corinthians 13 speaks of love so eloquently; it is "patient, kind, does not boast, is not proud or self-seeking. It is not rude. It keeps no record of wrongs, but rejoices with the truth. It always hopes, always trusts, always perseveres, and never ever fails." How can we go wrong if we do our very best to live out this definition of love? God's version of love is so much more perfect than ours. It isn't conditional or related to mood or whether or not you deserve it today. We are human and throw all sorts of other emotions into the pot like jealousy, for example. God's definition leaves no room for that nonsense.

We should pray with earnest hearts to love our spouses for who they are because in Christ we are all so much more! The years we spent together gave us tons of opportunity to trust God through challenges and trials. We will continue to grow in Him and change through the years. Our lasting love will not only be a legacy for our children but brings honor to a living God. I recognize that the youngsters we were at the start of our marriage are not the seasoned travelers you see before you now. In twenty more years, there will be even more change. This process takes decades but is worth the effort and prayer. So, what if I can't fit into my wedding dress?! I can still fit into my earrings from high school.

# Not Just a Job

S ome young people struggle to figure out what they want to do in a career for the rest of their lives. Many of them change major halfway through college. Unlike them, I always knew. From about age three, I knew. My mom had been injured at our home, and my dad wasn't home yet that evening. This was probably back around 1975 or 1976. We lived in East Tennessee at the time. Mom's sewing machine was out for repair, so she was borrowing one from a church friend. While carrying it in the case, the bottom fell out and the heavy machine crushed her toe and dented the wood floor beneath it. Not wanting a three-year-old to become hysterical, Mom wrapped her foot in a towel and sat in the kitchen, calmly calling my dad to come get her. In the meantime, she sent me to get her purse for her and some ice and other things I can't recall. The point was that I was helping in a stressful situation. She had been hurt. I was praised for being such a "big girl helper." That magical moment was when I knew helping others was my calling. I never strayed from my goal to become a nurse (unless you count that time I really wanted to sing professionally). And, no matter how musically talented I became during my teen years; I knew nursing was a paying job. Nurses could support themselves without a man if the right one never came along.

As a nurse, I've seen and done a great many things. I've done things, which go along with God's call to help in time of need and to love the unlovable. A nurse becomes the hands and feet of Christ. A nurse does for others at the worst times in their lives. I've cared for hurt and physically broken people and calmed their families. I've held the hands of someone dying and watched them take their final breaths. I've helped with resuscitative efforts, pulling someone from the edge where life and death meet. Caring and handling the most basic needs of being fed, clean, and safe is par for the course. Putting aside all bias can be difficult, but that's what nurses are called to do. Our ministry is in the way we show God's love for others. During His ministry, Jesus spoke specifically about taking care of the needs of others:

"For I was hungry and you gave me something to eat, I was thirsty and you gave me something to drink, I was a stranger and you invited me in, I needed clothes and you clothed me, I was sick and you looked after me, I was in prison and you came to visit me." Then the righteous will answer him, "Lord, when did we see you hungry and feed you, or thirsty and give you something to drink? When did we see you a stranger and invite you in or needing clothes and clothe you? When did we see you sick or in prison and go to visit you?" The King will reply, "I tell you the truth, whatever you did for one of the least of these brothers of mine, you did for me." (Matthew 25:35–40)

Now, don't misunderstand the difficulties of my job. In twenty-three years of nursing, I've seen negatives as well as positives. Patients and their families are not always gracious recipients of the care they receive. They can be messy, cranky, and otherwise foul, ruining a perfectly good day. I took care of a gentleman who was basically detoxing from prescription painkillers. During his stay at our facility, he was verbally abusive to the nursing staff and even threw feces at us. Another patient was verbally abusive when it took longer than usual to use a Hoyer lift to move her from the bed to a wheelchair. She weighed close to 400 pounds, and this was quite a difficult task for four staff members who were assisting. The comments she made offended me so greatly that for the first time in my entire career, I offered to have her assigned to a different nurse for the remainder of the shift. There is often condescension, hostility, or frustration, and nurses are easy targets to express all of these feelings. Despite this, I find great fulfillment and joy to balance out the negatives, and I've been blessed ten-fold for what I've done to help others. In one situation, a patient of mine cried at the time he was discharged from our care because he was afraid the next facility wouldn't take care of him in the manner that we had done. The simple joy of serving can be our greatest act of obedience. Each day brings unexpected blessings. I've taken care of people who are either angels or sent by God to inspire me to keep pressing on. I try to maintain a faithful routine of asking for God's guidance. Before I start each shift, I specifically ask God to bless my efforts and to show me ways and opportunities to serve others. For me, service goes beyond just administering medications and doing dressing changes on wounds. It means that when I'm able, I take time to know the patients and to share the love of Christ whenever possible. The opportunities to share Christ are really endless, and the ability to serve is an incredible gift.

# The Identifier

L et me first express that there is much prestige for the white coat worn by medical professionals. For five years I wore the coat as part of my job in nursing. Midway through this chapter of my life, I was given an opportunity to play a more impressive role, but it demanded more than I could give. The position I served in was important and related to new, ground-breaking heart procedures. For the first time in a long time, I felt important and needed. Over the course of several months, the job took more and more of my time. I put in a full forty hours, plus being at the beck and call of the director 24/7. If he decided to change something, I had to be ready to make those changes, even if it meant working from home after hours. I had to eat, sleep, and breathe this job in order to survive it. As time passed and the program grew, "mean girls" discovered that they could not change me, so instead, they drove me out. It began as playfully picking at me and progressed into full harassment. I was berated until I broke apart inside, my hands shaking with panic, and I couldn't function. I even lost weight. I was admittedly picked apart intentionally until I stepped down nine months later. My self-esteem was destroyed! At that moment, I should have quit. I should have gotten some therapy. Instead, I took a week off and let my employer place me in a new office, which was a terrible mistake.

Probably the larger mistake was letting my job title be my identifier. It's true that once you become a nurse, you are a nurse for life. You think and act like a nurse, even after retirement because it's engrained in you. This isn't necessarily wrong. After all, mothers are always mothers, and coaches are always coaches. Worldly success can be so appealing to us. The fancy title and the starched white coat make us feel terribly important. When we walk through the hospital, other people recognize us as someone of importance. Selfish ambition is all around us, and if we fall for that type of thinking, we set ourselves up for the worst kind of failure. We get wrapped up in simply trying to succeed and lose track of what's really important. When my job crashed and burned, I felt I was nothing. I had failed. This can happen so easily to anyone, and sometimes you don't even realize this is happening. My husband and kids felt they were second place, as well. Our relationships needed mending, and I needed to show them where my priorities lay. There went my big identifier. As Christians, a scenario like this can be incredibly damaging.

While in family therapy, my husband and I were asked to list the things that identified us. We had to come up with a list of twenty or more things that define us. This was tougher than I thought. Through this lesson, it became abundantly clear that my most powerful identifier should be "child of God." Wife, mother, and daughter fell closely behind that. What I do for a living is simply that. It's what I do when I can't be with my husband or kids, doing something together that we enjoy. I do still work as a nurse, and I really value the position I have to help people return to a healthy status, but now my job doesn't define me. This job doesn't require that I bring work home or completely consume my every thought. My husband and kids know every day how important they are to me, without question. This child of God doesn't eat, sleep, and breathe her job in order to survive. It's not my identifier.

# On Alert

As a registered nurse, I've worked in a variety of settings. I've worked inpatient, outpatient, clinic, hospital, and even procedures. And, in any of those settings, emergency situations can arise. Nurses are specially trained to detect when something is going horribly wrong and act accordingly, under the direction of a physician. We retake training for basic life support and advanced cardiac life support (ACLS) every two years to ensure we remain familiar with protocols and standard treatments. While I've been involved in code blue situations, I have participated in less than ten codes in my twenty-three-year career. Unless you work in the emergency room or in the intensive care unit, you seldom see a code. It's hard for these advanced skills to become second nature unless you use them frequently, so the renewal standard is every two years regardless of who you are.

The very first time I took the ACLS course, it was a horrible experience. My friend and I were fairly new nurses and working our first jobs right out of school. The protocols were unbelievable. At that point in time (twenty years ago), there was a great emphasis on knowing the dose of every drug and drip rate which could be used inresuscitation, plus the skills of defibrillation, cardioversion, intubation, and basic CPR (cardiopulmonary resuscitation). During class, you had the opportunity to practice the skill over and over until you felt comfortable. The class took up an entire weekend and was so stressful that even the men cried. I feared that if I couldn't memorize all the medication drip rates and algorithms for care, I'd never help save a life. Since then, I've renewed every two years, and have seen the guidelines change each time. The algorithms have been simplified to the point that there should be no need for stress. Yet, just the mere mention of an upcoming class, and I'm nervous again.

It's generally advised that medical staff not try to "cram" for the renewal. When I know my renewal is a couple of weeks away, I generally start reviewing material so that I'm prepared for class. Some otherwise experienced and intelligent people have failed because they waited until the last possible minute to study. In theory, the goal is to prepare medical staff for the worst event that could happen to anyone, which is cardiac arrest. A nurse may pass the class and carry the card but never ever experience a code blue during her career. It's not that we want to use these skills; the point is to be prepared at all times so that if duty calls, the nurse will act.

As Christians, we're instructed to be ready and prepared to share the Gospel in any setting and to be ready for Christ's return. "For you are fully aware that the day of the Lord will come like a thief in the night" (1 Thessalonians 5:2). No man knows when He will return. Being ready can't wait. Being ready means digging into your Bible as often as you can, growing stronger in your faith, and being prepared to share the Gospel at every opportunity. Being ready also means that you live every day as if it could be your last. According to scripture, He could return any time. If you're living in Christ, you have nothing to fear. Once again, this isn't like a test you try to cram for; this is lifelong learning between you and God. Christians need to gain the skills needed to utilize our very best source of help, Jesus Christ.

# Setting Limits

T oday, I'm sitting in the emergency room with a family and patient from my facility. The hospital I work at is great at lots of things, but we don't do diagnostic testing beyond a simple chest film. It's complicated. A nurse from our hospital typically travels in the ambulance across town to the ER and waits while a plan is formulated. Sometimes our patient is admitted, and sometimes they are treated and then return. You can never know what will happen or how long it will take. One time I rode with a transport after my twelve-hour shift and wasn't relieved by a night nurse until almost 11 p.m. That was a long day!

Today, I'm not bothered to be here with this patient. I'm on light duty (because of my recent arm strain), it's Sunday, and I didn't feel like being at work anyway. The only bothersome part about the situation is that I find it inhumane. Patients decline for all kinds of reasons. Lengthy illnesses, chronic pain, or multiple disease processes can exhaust a patient. Bedrest weakens them terribly. The drive to survive is a very powerful force. The drive to let go and disappear is even more powerful. There are tons of stories about elderly couples who were so connected and in love that when one of them passes away, the other soon follows. That's the way it is sometimes.

In the medical field, we're trained to save lives and to do good, not harm. We have advanced to the point that we can save almost anyone from anything. The ethical concern emerges from this basically good theory: given certain situations, sometimes doing everything is, in fact, the wrong thing. Advanced directives assist us in limiting life-saving interventions when it is appropriate to do so. A status of DNR or "comfort care" would prevent medical staff from performing any new or heroic measures to prolong the eventual outcome of death. I've always felt we should be as humane as possible in all situations. The flaw in the plan comes down to one word: family.

In twenty-three years as a nurse, I've seen every type of family dynamic you can think of. When patients are too debilitated to make their own decisions, the closest appropriate family members will make them. If a power of attorney (POA) is assigned, one person makes decisions; however, without a POA, there tends to be a lot more drama and even fighting about what is best. In this particular case, several family members were to meet with our staff on the patient's behalf, but no one showed up for the meeting. So, this elderly gentleman, too weak to sign papers or utter a complete sentence, remains a full code. I've stood at his bedside and held his hand. I've administered antibiotics. My coworkers and I have taken note of his unfortunate steady decline. Should his heart suddenly stop, medical staff will be performing procedures to restart it, even sending a current of electricity through his weak body. *If the family could only see what I see and know what I know.* If they did, they'd more easily let him go and not put him through these endless tests or procedures. But, if I weren't a nurse and didn't know all I know and if I hadn't seen so many things with my own eyes, I might be right there with them, asking him to just hang on.

Unrelated, but similar, the passing of any creature is a sad event. Our lab, Sandy, is now thirteen. She grew up with our children and has been an amazing family dog. She's the only pet my eighteen-year-old son has ever had, and she has been tirelessly faithful and loving. She let the kids hug and love on her as much as they wanted, especially when Bryan was gone for months at a time. She's licked the salty tears from their little faces and would then make rounds with me at night to check that the house was secure. She never barks unless she hears something, so I always felt extremely safe with her sleeping right next to my bed at night. These days, she has stiff hips and moves slowly. She's also blind in her right eye from a cataract. She has multiple lumps and bumps, which our vet assures us are harmless lipomas, but her newest lesion was concerning. I took her to see the vet and right away they suspected some kind of cancer. I declined the offer to biopsy the lesion, based on the fact that at thirteen, Sandy is the equivalent of a ninety-one-year-old woman. She also has a bad heart valve and mild congestive heart failure, but she's already outlived the average lifespan of a lab. If we're not planning to treat her for cancer, why do we need to know what the lesion is? The vet agreed.

Our once lively pal is becoming withdrawn. She hasn't chased a ball in about four years because of her vision. She remains happy and wags her tail, maybe four hours a day, but the rest of her time is spent napping. Occasionally, she appears depressed or worried and sometimes she shakes. Her once-hearty appetite has waned as well, and she prefers real cooked chicken and rice to kibble, but who wouldn't? Being the educated gal that I am, I've ordered books to read on the subject of pet bereavement. I'm serious. We know what the right thing to do is in this situation. We just need to know when to do it and how to handle it. Our family agrees that we don't want our sweet girl to suffer. It will be sad, but this is the circle of life. The plan is to take things one day at a time.

I have both a high school and a college graduate the same month and one child moving out for the summer (for the first time ever). This has provided a wonderful opportunity for my husband and me to really reconnect. Kids who are either moving out or have very busy schedules are seldom home, and both care for and entertain themselves. They have jobs and friends and are learning to manage with adult responsibilities. This leaves ample time for Bryan and me to either plan an evening out together or just some quiet time alone. It's typical that raising children can distract a couple from regular marriage maintenance, so this has been a great time for us. It's important to be on the same page with your spouse as you navigate new territory in your parenting. Having adult children doesn't mean they won't need you. They need you in different ways, even if it's just to listen to them verbally process something that they're going through. It's important that you are available to advise them and to pray for them constantly. Unfortunately, I keep cycling between pride in the kids because of their successes and pangs of sadness because of the emptiness I sometimes feel. Bryan assured me that if I ever got too sad, he'd take me for a ride on our Harley. I honestly love to ride on the back. He says there's nothing like the wind in your hair to get your mind off missing the kids. If we ride every time I fall apart, we might be putting a lot of miles on that bike! He's also so great about praying with me and for me, so I count on him as a partner in prayer. In a way, this is kind of like the very long honeymoon we never took, and it's for the rest of my life. So, where's my helmet?

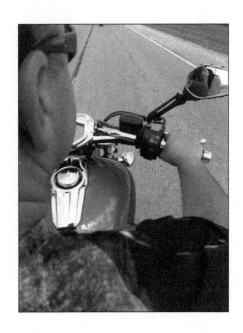

# Light Duty

I know I've explained before that I have always been accident-prone. In fact, growing up, my family joked that my middle name was "Grace" and not because I *had* any. Just about every injury I've had has been self-induced. Between my hip dysplasia, back issues since age nineteen, and frequent tendonitis I seem to develop from overuse, I've had everything from tennis elbow, sprains, rolled ankles, and so on. Once, I developed tendonitis of both my arms from simply bouncing a colicky baby for hours and hours (this was a very chunky baby). Occasionally, this requires a break from whatever activity has caused my injury. Lifting restrictions, ice or heat therapy, muscle relaxants, and anti-inflammatories are the name of the game sometimes. I've slipped on ice and fallen, or even tripped going *up* a flight of stairs in my attempt to do and handle everything in my life.

Currently, the ailment is my right elbow. On Christmas Eve this past year, I was walking down the sidewalk to deliver cookies to neighbors. Bryan and I made and decorated several dozen cookies for the joy of baking but planned to share most of them with friends in our town. Since it was unseasonably nice outside, I thought I'd walk to the houses I was delivering to. Not far from our house, I hit a slippery spot on the sidewalk, and before I knew it, cookie boxes went flying up and I came crashing down. I hit on my left hip and smacked my right elbow hard on the concrete. Not wishing to spend the holiday in the emergency room, I finished my deliveries and hobbled home to see what kind of shape I was really in. Over the course of the next twenty-four hours, I enjoyed some bruising to the hip and elbow but was able to move everything okay. I also had a mild case of whiplash, which was very annoying. A few days later, I felt fine. I managed to enjoy Christmas with our parents, and our daughter's boyfriend even came over for dinner. We all had a really nice time.

In late February, a confused 250-pound patient of mine man-aged to slide halfway out of the bed, but she was headed for the floor. Since we don't have an intercom system to call for help, my only appropriate action was to use the code blue button to summon the fastest help from coworkers. This was likely the initial strain which started my injury; however, it grew worse gradually over time with various activities. I likely have another tendonitis from overuse. Long story short: I'm on light duty. Light duty at my job means that I will not be assigned my own team of patients. I am not allowed to lift over ten pounds. I am allowed to function as a trainer/standby, but I can't wear a brace because it can't be sterilized between patients. There is a long list of duties that I am allowed to perform, which is good, but it doesn't feel quite as useful as taking a team and doing the physical part of nursing. Light duty for a month is going to get very old very quickly. Without being rude, I will have to gently remind my coworkers that I am not allowed to lift over ten pounds. I can, however, help in managing the unit I work on, which frees up the house supervisor to do her job more efficiently. I can spend time at the bedside with patients who need to talk with someone or need encouragement. There isn't always time for this level of attention when a nurse has a large team to care for. The entire shift feels like race against the clock.

On occasion, I encounter fellow Christians who are in our facility. The average stay at our facility is on average twenty-eight days. That's a long time to be away from your home and getting care around the clock. Most of the patients have already been in a short-term acute care setting a month prior to coming to ours, so they are tired and stressed out. Over the course of several days, I occasionally encounter a fellow believer who appreciates my offer to pray with them. One patient later introduced me to her spouse as "the nurse who prayed with me." This part of my job is very special, and I'll have more time to care for spiritual needs while on light duty. I'm happy to care for people in that way, and I consider it a personal mission to be the hands and feet of Christ and to be the girl who has time to recognize the concerns that they feel. This means everything! I'm trusting that God is going to put me in a position where I can be an influence, express the love of God, and encourage them during their struggle for wellness. God will use the situation these patients are in to reveal His bigger plan and to show His true nature as a loving, healing, understanding God.

I think this time on light duty is going to reveal some things to me about the true nature of God. I was thinking about different times in my life when my capacity to serve has been affected. Similar to my recovery from this recent injury, different seasons of life can alter our ability or availability. Maybe we have relocated, and people don't know us well enough to include us into a new church program or mission. Perhaps we haven't figured out where we fit in. Leaving a familiar church setting is difficult, and it's easy to feel lost until we are able to engage in close relationships like the ones we left.

Sometimes, something like being a new parent, sleep-deprived and stressed, can leave you with less energy to serve as you did before. Similarly, parenting young children can directly affect your ability to attend church, as illness may be frequent at your house. At the drop of a hat, someone can come down with sudden illness or situation that prevents you from fulfilling obligations or even attending church services regularly. It may be years before your church attendance and ability to volunteer to serve outside the home returns to what it was before. Honestly, parents of babies or young children are called to really concentrate their energies on the physical and emotional tasks of Christian parenting. Showing Christ through all you do and say at home has the greatest impact on your children, and for the first five years of their lives, their parents are their entire world. I can remember teaching my kids the song, "God is so good, He's so good to me" while I bathed them in the tub. I read them Christian bedtime stories, along with other traditional storybooks. Teaching them to pray before bed and at mealtimes is also a wonderful practice, but parenting young children is exhausting, and you need all the support you can get. Raising children who know Christ is far better than being spread so thin that you are too exhausted to meet the basic needs of your family. Christian parenting is perhaps the toughest job you will ever have, and it has an eternal impact. It is the most important job. God understands what life is like when you are raising your children. Similarly, a woman who has just lost her husband would never be expected to remain in her current level of service at church. This is a time in which a great deal of healing is needed. When a woman has a loss of this magnitude, there is no formula for how long it takes for life to feel "normal" again. This is a time when tons of support is needed, and service usually takes a back seat.

Many situations can make you feel you aren't pulling your weight in the Kingdom of God or make you feel like you are useless. You can't allow yourself to feel this way. In truth, there are a great many things which can sideline us in both attendance and service. Perhaps you have committed to be at the bedside of a family member who has been ill. Maybe a friend needs help you can provide. Sometimes, a mission we have helped with comes to a screeching halt for one reason or another. Satan would absolutely love for us to feel we are useless and dead weight to diminish the power of your testimony and influence. You cannot let him win this battle.

Not only are you serving by being a devoted mother, friend, or family member, but the reach of your personal ministry is actually expanding. Please know that your ministry is not diminished because of a different season of life you may be in. I think God occasionally shakes things up so that we can have a greater impact. Perhaps you have frequent medical appointments for physical therapy, chemotherapy, or some other issue. Your circle of influence has been totally changed, but you've just been placed in a different type of outreach. A new variety of people are in your circle, and you must be patient while God reveals His plan to use you. Your current situation may feel quite different and less comfortable than in past seasons. It may feel foreign to you and maybe you're not sure what serving Christ looks like in this new setting. God understands that each chapter in our lives looks and feels different, and maybe it's time for us to gain a new perspective.

The Bible says, "To everything there is a season" (Ecclesiastes 3:1–8). This passage is often used at funerals to remind us that even death is part of God's design. The loss of a loved one can impact others for Christ. Each season comes with different feelings; it expands our circle of influence and helps you and I reach many more for Him. Specifically ask God to reveal to you how He needs to utilize you. You'd be astounded at the blessings that flow in your direction when you get out of your comfort zone and express specific willingness to be used. God will provide exactly what you need to accomplish His mission. Please remember that you are never stuck, never useless, and never dead weight in the Kingdom of God. Light duty never means "off duty."

# Tales from the Campfire

As a pastor's kid, my childhood was dotted with annual summer trips to Christian service camp. It was always a refreshing break from an otherwise dull summer. I have so many camp memories. Camp was where I memorized most of the Bible scriptures I still know today. I remember how they would divide all the campers into groups, and each group tried to memorize as many scriptures as they could for points. The competition was fierce, as your status was announced several times a day, to promote more memorization and increased effort by the campers. We'd also compete for points during recreation times, giving points for winning a volleyball game or softball game. Each team wanted to win the pizza party (or whatever the prize was) at the end of the week for having the most points.

As exciting as my week of camp would be, it did create some anxiety for me. I had a stutter, which was worse when I was super excited or really revved up with sugar. Camp was full of all of these things, excitement, competition, and (at canteen time) sugar. My stutter was embarrassing, often making it a challenge for me to recite my Bible verses as effortlessly as other people. I was determined not to let it get in the way, and I was lucky that the adult sponsors were patient. Once I got going, I was fine. It was always getting out that first couple of words of the verse that had me stammering. Another cause of anxiety was mealtimes, not because the food was bad (often the food was terrific), but because dining hall shenanigans happened at every meal, and I didn't really want to be the center of attention. It was always a two-edged sword for me. You see, mail was distributed to campers during lunchtime. I hoped to get several letters from home while I was at camp. But, if a camper received three letters in one day or a package, they made the camper stand up in front of the whole dining hall and tell a joke in order to get their mail. Not only did I *not* know any good jokes, there was that whole issue of the stutter, and my anxiety level was through the roof! I longed for letters from home, but this hardly seemed fair in my opinion. I'd sit there during mail call in a full panic and couldn't relax until the whole thing was over.

I enjoyed the daily craft times, chapel, Bible study, and recreation. In general, I loved camp, and though I missed my family, I was making good friends who loved Jesus as much as I did. I always had such a tender heart, and at a young age, I felt that I should have been baptized much younger than I was. Back at my home church (where Dad was the pastor), I was living under quite the microscope. I had to be on my best behavior at all times so as to not embarrass my parents. I rarely drew negative attention and grew to hate the idea of it. I'd rather fly under the radar and not even be noticed than to draw any kind of negative attention. Going forward to accept Christ should have been such a great thing to do. Yet, the idea of walking down that very long aisle at our church grew increasingly more unappealing the older I got. As young as eight years old, I felt that I knew I was a sinner and was in need of forgiveness and grace. Often, a sermon or song would have my eyes full of tears, and I was emotional a lot of the time. Camp was great because the messages were more geared to my age group and understanding, although I was pretty mature for my age. The message of God's unfailing love hit home at camp, just like it did at my home church, but I still couldn't muster the courage to walk down the aisle. No matter how strongly inspired I was, my feet simply wouldn't move. It was as if they were encased in concrete.

I grew to love campfire time because at least in the darkness, no one could see my tearful expression, and it didn't draw attention. I could enjoy the crackling of the fire and the clear sky with stars above me, and let the message of God's love touch my soul. It was incredibly peaceful. You could hear the crickets when it was silent. Then, we'd sing praise songs a cappella and after that there would be a devotion and prayer before we walked back to the dorms for sleep. The year I turned thirteen was memorable for other reasons, though. Midway through my week of camp, several of us girls from my dorm saw something in the woods that scared the daylights out of us. We were on our way from the campfire to the dorm when several of us saw what we described as glowing green Jesus sitting on a tree stump! This was serious and completely changed every-thing. We were totally freaked out! Imagine a dozen twelve- and thirteen-year-old girls who believe in Jesus and are convinced that He has returned to earth. Throw some teenage hormones in there, and some procrastination about getting baptized, and you have a recipe for complete hysterics. Let's just say it took all the counselors we had (and two hours in the chapel) to convince this group of girls that we didn't miss the boat. One girl was so upset, she called her parents to come and get her. Two girls in the group were baptized the next day, and the remainder decided we would handle things at our home churches, after talking with our parents. This was an unusual event that no one could explain. How do a dozen girls have the same hallucination? All I know is that the residents of dorm number three thought they saw glowing Jesus in the woods and were scared they were all going to hell.

Campfire time was never the same after that, and neither was I. The mysterious sighting, which no one could explain, had indeed stirred urgency in the hearts of several campers. We learned that you shouldn't put off something that important because no one knows when Christ will return (for real) to take us all with Him to heaven. If this had been real, we would have heard trumpets and seen angels and people would have been rising upward, leaving even their clothes behind. Clearly, Jesus had not returned, but maintaining a state of readiness is as important as having a willingness to share the good news of Jesus with anyone at any time. I grew up a lot that summer. I also outgrew my stutter, and I learned a few jokes. No matter what the future held, I was going to be ready.

Bring on the mail!

# Detox

All over the media, we are flooded with information about taking our bodies through some type of detoxification process. Whether we are after weight loss or simply improving our general health, the programs available seem endless. Just last fall, I took myself through a detox to rid my system of sugar. I eliminated processed foods, dairy, and an entire list of foods, which are known to interfere with this process. I was warned it could be difficult and that I would likely experience annoying side effects like headaches, fatigue, or crankiness (watch out for that one). The program I was following had me replacing junk with better nutrients. I was also drinking some kind of a detox tea, which you can get at almost any grocery store. Determined to feel better and have more energy, I embarked upon a sixty-day fast from all sugar. Halloween came and went, and I think I might have had one piece of candy, which I don't consider to be failure. Not eating Christmas cookies was where I really struggled, which is why I gave most of them to people in our neighborhood. We kept a few at home, but a majority of them were enjoyed elsewhere. I think that during this time of detoxification, I felt focused and determined. Avoiding dairy was a great move and made me feel so much better physically. Eating less sugar and more protein gave me energy that lasted throughout the day, and since I was drinking all that tea, I was hydrated better than usual.

Unfortunately, it's not good to stay on a detox for very long. If you find you have food sensitivities, it's good to discover them so that you can avoid those foods in the future. But, though I eat a pretty balanced diet, I enjoy a sweet now and then and have a weakness for baked goods, which I have to really monitor. I was thinking just today about how a spiritual detox can be just as beneficial as a physical one. It's good for us to rid ourselves of things that clutter the mind or present distractions from following God. A spiritual fasting of the mind gives you opportunity to rid yourself of anything incoming that's not from God. Everything from our entertainment, radio station, friends, or other activities directly influences our relationship with the God who made us. Cut out, for a time, those things that hold us back from complete surrender and service. Evaluate what we are putting in so that everything we put out is representative of that relationship.

The best example I can think of would be a week a child might spend at a Christian service camp. Growing up, I attended at least a week of camp every summer. Granted, this was before cell phones and before the Internet, so there were far less things to distract us. Still, the list of things to leave at home included radios, video games, or anything that would be a distraction. You brought enough clothes for the week, bug spray, your sleeping bag, your Bible, and a notebook. That's it. You didn't usually bring all your friends from the neighborhood with you. You met new ones. There were outdoor activities like sports, chapel times, Bible classes, crafts, and always singing. My favorite time, however, was campfire. Unless it was raining, we had a campfire every night before curfew. Adults presented devotions, and there would be a time of prayer. Then it was time for bed, and you'd get up early to do it all again. The day your parents dropped you off, almost everyone got homesick. But, by the time they came to pick you up on Friday, you were crying because you didn't want to leave great friends. You just had the best detox week ever, in which the world did not influence you, and you were filled with the good news of Jesus! Everyone needs some time like this to shut out the world and detox. Unfortunately, you got back home to finish your summer, and soon the new school year started again.

As an adult with adult responsibilities, it's nearly impossible to arrange a week like this. You can't just drop your entire life and fly off to someplace secluded to think deep thoughts for a week. It's not practical in any way. We can take vacations, but this is the kind of time you need to take when it's just you and God and there are no other distractions. Since none of us can generally afford to disappear to a deserted island, I highly recommend finding a group of ladies with similar goals to hang out with on occasion. Make it a small group of two or three. Arrange childcare in advance and make it clear that you will be turning off your cell phone during this time (stay with me here; it'll be okay). Get together for a prescribed amount of time: maybe an hour. Bring your prayer concerns and pray together. You could meet at a local coffee shop or bookstore. Read a book by a Christian author and use this as a time to discuss each chapter as you go through the book. Study the scriptures. As our society becomes more engrained in technology as a way of life, it becomes more painful to unplug ourselves and detox. Start with this small block of time and devote yourself to standing by this method. Disconnect from the world and reconnect with God. Gain insight into the lives of a few close friends and share about how God is revealing Himself in each of your lives. Lift each other up in prayer and be encouraging. By regularly detoxifying, God will help you to become the best version of yourself, and you will function better in every other area of your life. Unplug from technology and plug into God.

# Forty-Something

**9** **a.m.:** I sat alone in Panera, enjoying breakfast and reviewing a local publication. To this day, I simply cannot sit alone in a restaurant unless I have something to read. It's one of my quirks, I suppose. I'd prefer to eat in my car rather than sit alone and have anyone assume I'm lonely.

Today's my birthday, and as I enjoyed my breakfast, I contemplated (carefully) my own evolution up to this point. At eighteen, I recall receiving a sewing machine from my parents and accused them of trying to "domesticate" me. Since that time, I've either crafted or sewn a dozen Halloween costumes or outfits for school plays, making each one with love. Similarly, when Bryan and I first married, my cooking skills were minimal. I only knew how to make four or five different dishes. I've come a long way in twenty-three years—thank goodness! I've become a purist of sorts, regarding

food. I either grow it myself or buy it at the farmer's market whenever possible. I'm far from an expert gardener, but I am learning
slowly, and I've canned things like salsa, jams, and green beans.

Before returning home, I made a couple of stops to do some
shopping. My mother had sent some birthday money, so I restocked
some of my favorite lotions and house sprays. I also shopped for a
new shirt to wear to an upcoming baseball game we have tickets to.
It was nothing major, but birthday shopping is always fun for me. I
called my mother on the way home to thank her for the gift and see
how she and Dad are doing this week. I think we talk once or twice
a week just to touch base with each other.

**10:30 a.m.**: I woke today to the beautiful sound of thunder and
rain, thankful that our garden and flowers were watered naturally.
When I returned from town, I began the chore of pulling weeds
and surveying the steady growth around me. My heart is thankful.
Gardening (though I'm not great at it) makes me feel somehow
closer to God. I'm always thinking of all the things He created for us,
and despite the eternal struggle with weeds, growing vegetables is
exciting! The soil was softened by the rain, so the weeds I pulled

came up easily, but by the time I called it quits, my shoes were caked in mud. I relocated to chores in the side yard, focusing on the black raspberry patch. Their season is quickly winding down, and the number of ripe berries is diminishing daily. It's been a couple of days since we picked some, so there was about a cup of berries to gather today. Ripe and juicy, they're protected by rather thorny bushes, which present a hazard. Over the past week, my arms and hands have looked more like I lost a fight with a cat. I remind myself that the season will be gone all too quickly, and it's worth it for the berry pie or jam I'll make from those berries. Growing things inspires me.

**3 p.m.**: I just might be unstoppable! I've had a nice lunch with Brandon, a short nap, and a refreshing shower. Bryan is home from work, and now our weekend really begins. A cup of coffee will perk me up, and I'll be totally ready for any birthday festivities. It's become increasingly more difficult to coordinate events with all of our busy schedules, but we do our best. Over the years, we have demonstrated the importance of family time to our children, so it's nice to see our young adults making it a priority. We maintain family supper as often as we can, sharing about our days and creating memories. We're diligent about carving out time to spend with one another. We realize the blessing of family should not be taken for granted.

Today I contemplate a life well-lived that is making an impact and leaving a legacy. There are just as many new challenges to face as there was when we brought our first child home from the hospital. I recently explained to the kids that as new parents, everything was new, and we were doing those things for the first time. With every age and stage of development, there were more new things to learn and additional challenges. Sometimes we got it right, and other times we didn't. Today, we may look like calm and cool experts, but we've never had adult children. This is another unique stage we're facing for the first time, and I guarantee we may make mistakes as we navigate new territory. Luckily, what was true in the beginning is still true: the same God who held our hands and walked beside us with new babies walks beside us to guide us through our current season. He didn't promise that any of this would be a cake walk, but He promised never to leave us. We can have security in the fact that our God will always be there.

**8 p.m.**: We were with wonderful people, wonderful pizza, and later there will be donuts. Nancy's Pizza is right next to Crispy Cream, and I'm not sure which I wanted more. We sat down and ate together (the four of us and Bryan's mother), and I was so blessed! It wasn't about the gifts I received but the sentiment in cards, which overwhelmed me. Later, freshly-made donuts would be an amazing treat and ending to the day. It was a beautiful evening and awesome birthday.

I need to backtrack, however, and explain how my amazing day actually started:

**6 a.m.**: It was my day off, so I had planned to sleep a bit late. My alarm went off, and as I rose to cross the room and hit the snooze button, I was suddenly aware of my first surprise of the day. My darkened bedroom had been lit up with several glowing balloons. I turned off the alarm and followed a trail of balloons out the bedroom, down the stairs, through the kitchen, and into the family room, where gold metallic balloons with "45" on them were hanging from the mantle. To add to this, each of the balloons had a message of love written in marker, saying things like "You're the best" or "We love you." I was speechless and incredibly encouraged by these

messages of love. I'm not sure how these years went by so quickly

or how we made it to this point, but I like this stage very much, and

I know it's a day blessed by God Himself.

# The Journal

Sharon, my mother-in-law, is many things. She's a retired licensed practical nurse (LPN), mother, grandmother, and a close personal friend. After the passing of Bryan's father in February of 2012, she shared with me a journal in which she tells the story of her life up to the present. I felt so privileged have read it and found it touching and inspiring. She wrote of her life growing up, how she met Bryan's dad, and of their life together. There were parallels between her life and mine in that she instantly knew that she and Butch were meant to be together and that their initial meeting was followed by a year-long separation. They only went on a handful of dates before Butch left for Viet Nam. While apart, they wrote letters almost daily for a year. Bryan, my husband, left for Korea after we'd had only three dates. While the men were gone, we each got to know their extended families quite well.

Sharon and Butch lived a happy life, raising three kids in a small town, until Butch was diagnosed with leukemia. He suffered through eight months of rough chemotherapy and nearly died. He spent sixty-four days in a coma after the last round, and it literally took a miracle from God to heal his body. The testimony of faith I read sent chills up my spine. Prior to this illness, Butch had not been living for God. Knowing that there was only one way he could be healed, he got on his knees beside his hospital bed and gave his life to Christ. After his healing, their testimony was shared with many, through visiting churches and speaking about this miracle. Butch was given twenty-five extra years and spent all of them free of cancer. Since he was medically retired from the railroad, he served in many other ways. He served as the building manager for their church, handled all the mowing and maintenance, and gardened and grew all kinds of things at home. The story of Butch and Sharon's incredible love and also the love of God is inspiring. The lifetime kind of love is honestly a gift straight from God Himself, and if we are lucky, we find this kind of love.

I never knew Butch prior to his cancer. The Butch I met in the fall of 1992 had been transformed. His voice was raspy due to being intubated during that sixty-four-day coma. His vocal cords had been scarred. His gait was uneven because of drop foot he developed in the intensive care unit. He had a bit of hearing loss (okay, a lot of hearing loss) from the chemotherapy. But, still in his forties, he was a skilled man who took care of his family and kept plenty busy. He was a kind and godly man and living proof of the power of prayer. As a father-in-law, Butch was wonderful! He was a reliable voice of reason. He shared his lifetime of experience with his children and his grandchildren, guiding them with a warm hug and understanding. He could be very reassuring, and if he put his hand on your shoulder and told you something was going to be okay, you believed it. Butch was always looking to preparation for the future, advising on the sound investments of home and family but rarely talking about the past. He'd tell you all you wanted to know about relatives now gone but not about Viet Nam. It changed him in ways we'll never know. He was a man of prayer and faith and encouraged his family to have faith as well. Knowing that you were on his prayer list was an incredible compliment. I happen to know he prayed for me.

Butch was busy and always working; he believed in honest labor and in doing for others. He took care of his mother and sisters for years, being there to mow or fix things. He never considered it a burden to handle finances or manage the business of his family. He could build almost anything, and when it came to growing things, he had a green thumb for sure. He loved to take people out in the yard and show them everything he had growing. He was also generous in sharing plants, giving many to Bryan and me for our new home.

In February of 2012, Butch passed away suddenly. It was unusually warm and pleasant for that time of year, but he had plans to cut down a small tree in the front yard. Sharon took off in the car to pick up a grandchild for a sleepover. She would come home to find him lying in the grass behind the tailgate of his little truck. He had already laid the chainsaw in the bed of the truck and an elderly neighbor had been watching him with binoculars out of sheer curiosity. He reportedly sat down on the lawn, and then lay back flat. After a moment, when the neighbor didn't see him get back up, he called 911. Sharon followed the ambulance into her own driveway, not knowing what was ahead. He was only sixty-three. During preparation for his funeral services, mysterious things began to happen. We honestly believed Butch was still with us somehow. In going through his closet, seven brand-new Cardinals baseball t-shirts were found. Each of seven grandchildren had a shirt for the visitation to honor Grandpa's favorite team. Then, there was a song list found on his laptop computer. The song list was strangely appropriate for his funeral. We couldn't explain any of these things, except to say that he was really a planner.

Butch is visible to me in many ways. I feel him with me when I'm working in my garden and when things are nicely growing. I remember him when I look around our house and see all the projects he had helped with. When a cardinal flies around my yard and hangs around, I think about him. There are times that remembering brings tears, but mostly it brings a smile. Life's lessons are hard sometimes. I think if there's a lesson to be learned through his passing, it's that life is short. You never know how your days here are numbered, so be as good to those you love as you can possibly be. Live in the faith of a God who is bigger than all the pain, and don't take anything or anyone for granted. Butch was a great example of enjoying every moment whether out in a fishing boat or in the garden.

The journal Sharon wrote is meant to be shared and will hopefully be read by many. Her love for God is evident, and she writes it as an invitation to anyone far from Christ. Sharon experienced signs and wonders directly from God, and I believe her mission is clear. The Bible says, "Blessed are those who have not seen and yet believe" (John 20:29). Sharon saw God's mighty hand in the healing of her husband when cancer almost took his life. The additional twenty-five years we had with him were icing on the cake. Butch was a blessing to anyone who knew him. He was definitely a blessing to me. When we devote our lives to living for God, we leave a legacy behind. The creepy coincidence of the baseball shirts and the songs on his computer, simply remind me that not only is heaven very close, but God is always in the details. There was a great deal of comfort found in the way things just worked themselves out.

# Stranger

I grew up as a pastor's kid and in a sort of proverbial bubble. My parents did their best to provide a godly influence at all times. I was never exposed to smoking, drinking, or dangerous behaviors. I was in church every Sunday unless I was seriously ill and rarely ever went to a babysitter's. Mom stayed home with us until both my brother and I were in grade school, and I grew up assuming every other family in America was just like mine. I also assumed that even if we didn't get along perfectly all the time, my only sibling and I would always be in each other's lives. The harsh reality is that all families interact differently. Every household has a different dynamic. Parenting styles are not identical, and for that reason, I found it stressful to even go on sleepovers as a child. Not everyone stays together for a lifetime. Sometimes members of families fall out of that relationship and drift away. Family ties don't always remain tied, and hearts are often broken. We're all human, and humans make mistakes. We don't always extend grace and forgiveness to each other the way that we should, and the result can be devastating. The same year I married my husband, my grandparents divorced after decades of a life together. I had assumed they would always be together. That was a fantasy. I faced a harsh reality that the safe little world I grew up in was far different than the world around me. I had to accept that my family wasn't perfect, but it would be years before the ultimate fall-out would shake me up. I never stop praying, however, that God will reunite all of us again.

As a mother of two kids, I can attest to how shockingly different two children can be. I'm amazed all the time at my own children and how each have their own strengths and weaknesses. From the moment they were born and their personalities emerged, they were unique and unlike anyone else. Parenting them has been not only an adventure but a privilege, which I'm daily thankful for. I also find it fascinating, watching my kids go through so many phases and stages. Mine are right on the cusp of adulthood and independence, and the teen years have brought just as many adjustments as toddlerhood. I've read articles on raising responsible kids that agreed that kids do just as much changing during the teen years as they did between ages two and four. It's an honor to help Laina and Brandon develop the skills they need to manage adult responsibilities. Of course, we're taking baby steps, but in general things are going well.

Looking back to my household growing up, I see so many parallels. My brother was three years younger than me, and our family did a lot of moving around. From very early on, he was disadvantaged. He was placed in glasses at age five, had few friends, and was picked on all through grade school. I remember back in the late 1970s when parents left kids in the car alone while they went into the grocery store. Mom had left us both in the car, and my brother cried so hard about it that he actually threw up in the car! Despite my pleas for him to stay with me (so we wouldn't get into trouble), he got out and went into the store to find her. A bit later, the two of them returned to the car, and I don't recall him being reprimanded. Although I could be a real attention seeker, I hated negative or unwarranted attention. I kept to myself in uncomfortable situations, while my brother would be hanging out the car window, waving at total strangers.

My brother was different. From the day he arrived in that white bassinette, I resented his presence. I was the child who was pressured to be perfect, while my brother was raised more loosely. He was cute and overly energetic to the point that people would comment, "Maybe he needs medication." I recall a great aunt of ours spouting something to that effect when he was about four. I decided at that moment not to like her or ever hug her because of that comment. I felt defensive and wondered how she could be so insulting! I was maybe eight at the time. As a child, I did not understand what was really going on. All the moving that we did would prove problematic by the time he was in about the third grade. He was difficult to manage and unpredictable at best. Mom and Dad got lots of calls, and over the years he was tested for vision and hearing difficulties but never for ADHD. If we'd been in any school system long enough to raise the red flags, I'd like to think that an intuitive teacher would have suggested testing. The year I was in sixth grade, my brother would have been in third. We were in three different schools that year. I was an average student and managed to pass; however, my brother would be held back for material he definitely missed. This was unfortunate, but a smart move to repeat this grade.

As we grew up, I think the competition for attention was intense. I was a B student and stayed busy with choir, theater, and music. I was generally very good at all of that. I helped with the house and laundry and tried not to draw negative attention to myself. The polar opposite of that is the child who feels they must compete for equal attention. If they can't get it by being better than you, they'll try to get it for being bad or doing things that are shocking. I can't tell you how many times my brother either shaved his entire head or dyed his hair some weird color for attention. This was his approach to life. Even bad attention was attention. He struggled in school, which should have been a sign that something bigger was wrong. I remember many nights both of my parents sitting over him at the kitchen table yelling at him about finishing homework, and it took all three of them some nights to get that stuff done. There was so much drama and yelling! I'd shut myself in my room and do my own homework with headphones on so that I couldn't hear them. It was upsetting to me. Dad finally contacted the school board and demanded that some type of evaluation be done to figure out what was wrong. My brother was seventeen when the diagnosis of ADHD was finally given. The school felt it was too late to start medication and after meeting with some type of therapist, they decided it was best to treat for depression. Had my parents known what types of help were available to him (that are mandated by the law) things could have gone so differently. This was all happening in the 1980s and '90s, before the Internet was at our fingertips. When he received his high school diploma, I honestly thought Mom and Dad should have walked across that stage with him.

The research I did to help my own child would have been so helpful to my parents. It's very typical that kids with untreated ADHD experiment with alcohol or drugs in order to find some level of total focus. Knowing this, I was determined to help my child as young as possible to perhaps avoid this issue. Through conversation, I found out that it was a school counselor who made the suggestion to my brother that using marijuana could help him focus. I'm understandably angry. There are so many reasonable modalities, which could have helped him be successful during those growing-up years. The type of accommodations suggested for ADHD or other disabilities differ, depending on your age. Small children qualify for a teacher's aide in the classroom to physically monitor them. Any timed test can be administered untimed. If the presence of extra noise or the classroom crowd is too distracting, the child can be pulled into another room where it's totally quiet and they are alone to finish the task. The use of tape recorders is encouraged, as they may "space out" during a lecture and miss valuable material. Independent tutoring is also an option available.

And, typical of all ADHD, it affected (and continues to affect) every type of relationship my brother had. ADHD kids lie about obvious things. With chocolate on their faces, they'll insist that they did not eat the last donut. They cannot sit still for any length of time without constantly tapping a foot or a pencil on a table. They are forgetful. Dating is difficult because they easily lose interest. Sugar intake intensifies hyperactivity, but stimulants (like caffeine) cause relaxation. He could drink a double espresso and go to bed an hour later with no difficulty. Maintaining friendships (or any relationship) is hard for them. They will lie to you, steal from you, and generally disappoint you. If we had only known how we could have helped him. Back then this issue wasn't as widely known as it is today. The methods my brother chose to cope led him down a more unsavory road. He caused my folks many sleepless nights and heartache. What kills me is that he was hurting, too. I feel that in the end, he had unmet needs from a very young age and that things would not be as they are today if those needs had been met.

Bryan, my husband, has two siblings. While they may not agree on every topic, they have an incredible thing in common: they shared a childhood that they can reminisce about. I've sat at family gatherings, hearing stories of adventures they had or crazy things they did as kids and wished that my situation were similar. I shared my childhood with one person. Sadly, we are estranged. How I'd love to sit around with him and chat about the things we both remember—the many moves, new places, and interesting people. We tried that once. During a move from Alaska to North Dakota, we traveled to visit both sides of the family. Bryan's parents and family were in Illinois, and my family was living in Michigan. My brother had moved up there when Mom and Dad moved and had met a great girl who was a hairdresser. They had been married for about four years when we made this trip, but I had never met my sister-in-law in person. The year they married, we were living in Arkansas and our son, Brandon, was due to arrive in about a month. My doctor wouldn't let me travel for the wedding. This was our first chance to meet, and I was really excited. Things didn't go as I imagined. Bryan and I went out with my brother and his wife for bowling and to visit at a small pub. Over the course of the evening, I learned of damaging things, which happened to my brother as a child. He said negative things about my parents, and I was left incredibly hurt. I described it later as "parent bashing." I was left so insulted and hurt by the things I heard that night. Bryan and I lay in bed quietly discussing the encounter, and at one point I shared those hurtful things with Mom. This began an unfortunate relay of e-mails between Mom and me over several months, in which she asked me for advice in getting along better with her daughter-n-law. It was wrong for us to talk about her. Mom had, had this wonderful idea that they would develop a relationship like the one she and I had shared for years, but it wasn't to be. We are very different, and she comes from a different kind of family. Mom's need for advice was innocent, and my wish to help her was also innocent. There was no intent to cause harm or hurt. I wanted to help my mother cope and nothing more. Favors she did (like leaving bagels and the Sunday paper on their stoop) were viewed as stalker-like. Most people would have thought that was a sweet gesture from a sweet person but not my brother and his wife. What a strange situation.

The nail in the coffin was when my brother hacked into my mom's email account and read the months and months of e-mails we had written. As stated earlier, our intent was innocent. The content of those e-mails destroyed any hint of trust we might have had between us and would flavor every encounter we had over the next decade. On the surface, we were all getting along, but that bitterness from mistrust reared its ugly head. During the seven years we lived in North Dakota, I would get a phone call from my brother about twice a year. Any call I made to him went automatically to voicemail. We'd keep the conversation light, and inevitably he'd start in with something hurtful, and I'd spend the next two days crying. This cycle repeated until 2012. In attempt to try to reconcile, I had invited him to see his niece star in the school play. At first, our correspondence was positive and things felt okay, but it soon took a turn from which there is no recovery. He called me on my cell at work, which was a surprise. Knowing that we seldom talk, our secretary encouraged me to step into our doctor's private office and chat with him. He must have been under some kind of chemical influence because he let loose some harsh and hurtful words and had me in tears! I was crying so hard that I was asked to leave work early that day. I found out that this type of thing frequently happened to Mom because he would call her up either drunk or high and verbally abuse her, blaming her for everything wrong in his life. He'd use foul language and spout long, seemingly rehearsed rants over the phone. It had just happened to me, and it was appalling!

As earlier stated, every single relationship in my brother's life is affected. He would have difficulty keeping jobs, and it would take him a long time to complete college courses. Add to this the very real possibility of mental illness and continued substance abuse, and you have a recipe for disaster. I don't know how he is today or even where he is. I made the necessary choice to eliminate all means to contact him. To my knowledge, he doesn't accept calls from our parents or other family members. This isn't how I imagined my life would be. I hoped that we'd have a relationship similar to the one my husband's family shares, but this is not to be.

My parents returned to Illinois after nine years in Michigan, probably a decade ago. We see them as often as we can. To my knowledge, my kids are their only grandchildren. The heart-breaking truth is a difficult pill to swallow. I accept that I contributed to the wall between my brother and me. However, given what I've learned since that time, I feel it would have happened anyway. The situation we are in is indeed a cruel one, and it pulls no punches. I may never understand what caused this turn of events, and I wish we could go back in time and fix what's clearly broken. I am no longer that sassy twelve-year-old sister who probably hurt his feelings. I'm a mother of two grown children who knows how important the sibling relationship truly is. In fact, I use my situation as an example of how things can go wrong and encourage my kids to not end up we did. During that brief time before the final blow, he used social media to contact both Brandon and Laina. I had planned to talk with them about it being their choice to have a relationship with their uncle. He beat me to it, and they had already resolved that it wouldn't work for them. Wow! I was impressed at their maturity and very thankful.

I believe strongly in the power of prayer, and I believe that God cares about even the tiniest detail of our lives. The best and only plan of action for a situation like this is to let God handle it. I dream of a day when my doorbell rings and my brother is standing there. I'm fully prepared to greet him with open arms, but I honestly don't feel that day will ever come. My most recent experience with him, while terribly unsavory, led me to believe that something went terribly wrong. I wasn't able to get a word in, much less reason with him. My parents assure me that there is no reasoning. This is such a huge worry for me; sometimes it consumes me. I pray that God will bring healing. For the first time ever, I was asked about him, and I simply stated that we aren't in each other's lives. He decided not to be a part of our family. It's taken me years to be able to say that. Sometimes, it works to think of myself as an only child. His birthday always makes me sad, and it's as if I'm remembering someone who has passed on. I once wrote a poem (which I failed to find) where I wrote that he traveled to where I could not reach him. Clearly this is true. I can't reach out, and if I could, it might not be pretty. One thing that will never change is that I'm his sister and I love him. I pray that God can fix what's broken and bring him back to me.

I find it somewhat reassuring that the longer I live, the more people I meet who share this similarity with me. I've met several people over the years with estranged siblings or strained family bonds. I think as children, we live in a bubble. All we know is our family and how our family functions. It was years before I was exposed to various types of dynamics. As a child, I enjoyed the predictable structure of my family, and any setting outside of that made me very uncomfortable. Something as simple as a sleepover at my cousin's house would make me upset. The parenting style in their home was dramatically different and extremely laid back. There were several times she wanted me to stay over, and I just cried and cried. I couldn't explain at the time that the whole thing made me uncomfortable.

At some point, we come to label systems, which don't work correctly as "dysfunctional." These systems stray from the accepted norm. Whether we are measuring the system against our own standards, society's standards, or God's, there's something wrong. Of course, the ultimate standard for our lives is God's word. Interestingly, there are dysfunctional family units throughout the Bible that demonstrate God's use of imperfect people to carry out His perfect plan. Cain and Abel (in Genesis) had differences. Their story is one filled with lies, deception, and murder. Mary and Martha in the New Testament differed in what they valued. One sister was cleaning house and preparing to make a good impression, while the other was at the feet of Jesus. The story of the prodigal son tells of a boy who took all his inheritance and blew it living wildly. After he hit rock bottom, he was still able to return to a loving father who threw a party at his safe return. Joseph (Genesis) was sold into slavery by his eleven brothers because of jealousy over favoritism. Through study you can find many examples. All of these stories bring me reassurance. I am reassured that my situation is not the worst in the history of all mankind (although sometimes it feels that way). I am also assured that with every situation, God will work all of it out for good and to bring Him ultimate glory. I also know that God cares about every detail of my life, and He cares about this dysfunctional relationship as much as I do, if not more.

Once again, my best advice is pray, pray, pray!

# Fearless

My daughter's initial employment after completing culinary school was a full-time job at our local Christian service camp as the head morning cook. She was so excited to be living at the camp and working in an environment that would foster her Christian growth and her cooking skills. Prior to the start of the camp season, the entire staff took part in a wilderness experience where they go far out into the woods and tent camp for a few days. A scheduled activity is the crossing of a rope course high above the ground. It would be intimidating and challenging, but an exercise in faith and trust that went beyond just physical strength. Mental and emotional strength were also required, along with a simple willingness to participate.

Laina was focused and determined. This was new territory for her. The challenge to get across a rope course twenty feet above the ground was daunting. Her safety harness was secured, the rope was taut, and her friend was calling to her from the other side of the obstacle. Things were going all right until she was two-thirds of the way across. She reached for the next rope and then lost her grasp. She immediately panicked! The fear of death washed over her as she hung there, unable to pull herself upright. Twenty feet felt more like two hundred.

In that moment of fear, Laina was thinking about the twenty-third Psalm, especially the part about "walking through the valley of the shadow of death." She tried to remember all the tips that were reviewed before this climbing activity: (1) Keep your eyes focused on the step you are on; (2) use the safety words; and (3) don't look down. Everyone tackles the rope course differently. Not everyone places their feet or hands on the same spot. Some are quicker than others, and some fearlessly hang from the ropes like monkeys. Braver folks even tackled the higher course, which was forty feet above the ground. It's not uncommon to momentarily slip and then regain your grip. In extreme cases, a rescue is required, as was required for Laina.

Despite her inability to recall the exact details of her rescue, Laina learned a lot about herself through this activity. She was assured that being rescued did not mean she failed the course. Her simple willingness to participate, though heights scare her immensely, showed great inner strength and maturity. Later, she would share with me that the course was rather symbolic of several things in her own life and held deeper meaning. The difficulty of the course might either represent our lives in Christ in their entirety or merely a portion of time in which we face great trials. The obvious uncommon truth is that life is full of trials and difficulties, and we are called to "consider it pure joy when we face trials of many kinds, because you know that the testing of your faith develops perseverance. Perseverance must finish its work so that you may be mature and complete, not lacking anything" (James 1:2–4).

We're promised in Deuteronomy 31:6 that God will never leave us or forsake us. Just like Laina's safety harness on the rope course, we're secured in Christ and have that added protection. We are never alone no matter what we face during our lifetimes. The most important thing she learned was that moving forward in her walk with Christ was a lot like the course and is a universal truth;

Individuals may be unsure of where to place their hands or feet on the rope, but we serve a living God who is in complete control. Not only does He hold us in the palm of His hand, but He's waiting for us at the end of the course.

# Ella

Grandmother Ella was someone very special to me. Growing up, our family lived at least an hour from any relatives. Typically, we would visit grandparents and extended family a couple of times a year. With that in mind, a visit to see Grandma was a special event and one that meant a lot to me. She lived on a farm as far back as I can remember, and I loved being able to wander off to explore on the property. Grandma grew things and made things and was always doing something for someone else. She was very special to me, and she loved all of her grandchildren.

When I think of her, I think of a photo we used for her eightieth birthday party invitation. Her favorite color was lavender, so we chose lavender cardstock and adhesive crystals to create the most precious announcements. In the photo, a young girl walks alongside her bicycle. She has a smile on her face, and the wind blows her hair softly. Her style is appropriately from the 1940s, and she is sixteen and beautiful. What I know about my grandmother's life was confirmed for me in a journal my mom found. She began writing about her childhood back in 2010. This was after she moved into an assisted living facility and prior to her rapid decline from dementia.

Through the journal and stories, I learned that my grandmother had Cherokee heritage. She was born in a schoolhouse in White City, Illinois. Her journal states that she never knew the full story of her family but was told that her mother passed away when she was only two months old from a ruptured appendix. She had two older sisters and an older brother, whom her father continued to raise. But he was an alcoholic and overwhelmed with a new baby. Her grandma Osborn would make the decision of what to do with her, so she was given up to an aunt and uncle. All her close relatives had large families of eight to twelve children, but Osa and Sarah Davis had none. Her father eventually remarried and had several children, giving Grandma several half-brothers and sisters. Many of her cousins attended school with her in Hornsby, but she wrote that she didn't know any of them very well. Her foster parents strongly discouraged her from associating with her siblings and half siblings, which made her very sad. Grandma wrote in her journal about how the entire extended family would get together twice a year, gathering for a picnic at the cemetery where their loved ones were buried. Memorial Day was always an annual get together.

Grandma walked one mile to school every day, unless it was raining. If it was raining, she could get a ride to school on her Uncle Roy's milk truck. Roy hauled milk to the Litchfield creamery every day. She loved living in the country. Her family put out a thirty-acre garden and had cows, chickens, and horses. Growing up, she learned to cook, clean, can, sew, and all basic skills for life. At ten, she was put in charge of feeding and watering the chickens and picking up the eggs. She wrote about naming all of the animals on the farm and how they were her pets. She named everything! There's a funny tale in her journal about how a rooster gave her a hard time, and she hit him with a 2 x 4, seeming to knock him out. She ran back in to tell her mother she'd killed him and was immediately instructed to go and gather all the eggs. After gathering eggs, she found that same rotten rooster waiting for her outside, ready for another fight! Grandma appreciated what she had, and while she never received allowance for her chores; she had food, clothes, and a place to sleep. She wrote about being thankful for a roof over her head. There was so much to be done on the farm that she was never bored. This explains why she'd get so flustered with her own grandchildren if you ever came up to her and complained that you were bored. She would *really* give you a piece of her mind. When Grandma was ten, her mother developed arthritis in her hands, and she had to take over milking cows. She wrote that her goal was to be able to fill a milk bucket faster than her father. Eventually, she reached that goal, and it made her very happy. She wrote a lot about raising chickens, hatching new baby chicks, and how beautiful it was to pick up a fuzzy, yellow chick for the first time. She loved their warm fuzziness and that cute little "peep" that they made when she picked them up.

Grandma was a big fan of Shirley Temple, growing up. Her journal states that they were the same age. While her family never had a Christmas tree, they did surprise her with a Shirley Temple doll, which she wanted more than anything else in the world. She had no idea how they afforded to get it for her, but she received it, along with the standard coloring book and crayons she got every year. Birthdays were celebrated with only a small cake or some cookies. She wrote about her Uncle Roy, never forgetting her birthday, however:

> Uncle Roy would always remember any birthday. When I walked home from school, I went past where he kept empty cans left by the milk hauler. If one of the lids was sitting on crooked, I knew he remembered. Sure enough, there would be candy or cookies in there. If there were two, then I was one happy little girl!

Probably the most interesting story in her journal is the story about a tornado from 1938. Grandma was ten at the time:

> When I was ten years old in 1938 we had a bad tornado to come in the evening on the last day of March. I never knew what Dad was talking about until it was over with. Of course, there were no electric wires or telephone wires, but this happened around 7:00 in the evening. The lightning was bad before

the storm, and Dad went to the barn to let the cows and horses out—not knowing what kind of a storm this was. We always had a lot of thunder, lightning, and wind. When he got back to the house, he locked the kitchen door and placed a wooden chair under the doorknob, and he said, "It's coming!"

All at once the wind was strong, and our house was just four rooms with porches on the south and north. We went in the back bedroom to have as many walls to protect us as we could. It took every window out of our home. It took the chimney off the top of the house and the porches off. We were in the bedroom down on our knees, and Mom and I were praying to God, but I could not hear Dad praying. My little dog was under the bed, as she was afraid, too. It seemed like it was hours, but it was only a few minutes. The storm had come from the southwest from Bunker Hill. Since we didn't have a radio, we knew nothing about it.

After the storm was over, we had boots on and were walking in about a foot of water inside our house. With the windows all out, it was raining in. Momma soon hung blankets over the windows to keep the cold out. The rain came down the stovepipe and ruined Momma's kitchen stove. The next day, Dad walked to Litchfield to buy a new stove. The chicken house was gone, and so were the chickens. The old barn was half-gone, but our old storm buggy and a little room where Mom had two setting hens sitting were all right. The old hens set on their nests and hatched out chickens. These were the only ones we had left. God does provide a new start! Our cattle were fine. They were afraid, but they all lived. One of Dad's horses died. There was tin off the outbuilding wrapped in trees for years to come. One of our outside dogs died, and every time it looked like rain with thunder and lightning, it made me nervous.

We saw Uncle Roy, Uncle Sherman, and Aunt Blanche going to the storm cellar. Uncle Roy was lucky to be alive. The wind had taken him over. We had a lot of building to do and a garden to put in, but we weren't alone. Dad's brother and sister lived on the other hill. They built a storm cellar on the east side of the hill, and when a storm came up you could run to the hill. Uncle Roy took hold of a little bush on the hill and said he could see everything going over his head: animals, cows, boards, and tin from roofs. He was safe hanging on the little tree on the east side of the bank. The old house they lived in was the old family homestead. It had some windows out and the roof was off. After the storm, our folks would take lanterns and call to the folks to find out if they were all right.

I could not find my old chicken Aunt Blanche gave me. The storm had blown a hay pile into the road we drove up to the house. One of our dogs was under the hay pile for two days, and then he finally came home. I always had a box on the back porch for him, so when the porch blew off, so did he.

I was so happy to see him, and I think he was happy, too, and hungry. Some things we never found, and other things we found all summer long! Great big trees were pulled out of the ground. I know God watched over us.

During the last couple years of her life, I would hear more stories about her childhood than ever before. Sadly, Grandma had been diagnosed with Louis body dementia, and her reality was all about the past. It was fresh in her mind, and she loved to share. She never finished high school and never had a driver's license until into her twenties. She walked to school in the snow, attended class in a one-room schoolhouse, and her parents were especially strict. Her dad didn't tolerate whining or children who couldn't entertain them-selves. In fact, he could be terribly unreasonable most of the time. It was his opinion that the wife of a farmer didn't need a high school diploma. Some of this explains why Grandma was so intolerant of whining or drama.

Grandma met my grandfather in 1947. In her journal, she writes:

I met my wonderful husband at my Uncle Wes Davis' farm sale. Francis was a handsome Italian farmer from Gillespie. We went together for one year and were married on Sept 7, 1948. We lived at Gillespie for six months. Then Dad became sick so we moved back to Walshville. We all lived together until our family started to grow and we decided to build a new house.Ella and Francis Caesar Genta had five children. My mother is the eldest daughter and the second eldest child. When Mom was about thirteen, they divorced. This left her with five kids and a good-sized farm to run all alone. Without a high school diploma, Grandma did all kinds of things from taking in laundry and sewing to selling the eggs from her chickens. She would later be hired as a dietary aide at the local hospital until her lack of education would phase her out. She cleaned houses later on until she was too old to drive or work.

The farm near Sorento, as I recall, was large. There was always a huge garden, fruit trees, and room for chickens. Her second husband, who I don't really remember, was a help with the farm but was completely nuts and nearly burned the house down. Husband number three, Clarence, came along when I was about seven and was honestly the sweetest of the three. He put in a pond, was tolerant of Grandma's many moods, and made her incredibly happy. The two of them remained on the farm until the upkeep became too much to handle with too many acres to mow. In their seventies, they sold the farm and moved to town but were never really content. There was one more attempt at country life a couple of years later, but as health and finances declined, depression set in. Clarence took his own life. Within three years, Grandma would be in an assisted living facility, and the remainder of her story would play out like that of so many others. There would be a slow and steady decline until she left this world herself.

Grandma was a depression baby. She was a pack rat and kept everything you can imagine. She didn't grow up with much, so she threw out nothing. Her inability to part with scraps of material or other items made it difficult to relocate her to a facility. My mother would spend days going through things and getting things ready for donation because she would be living in a small space with no storage. Up until one year before her passing, she was still reading books and doing crochet. Mom made sure she had plenty to read and things to do. Soon, the dementia would make her forget her crafts, and reading and other interests would fade.

The last memorable visit I had with Grandma was about a year prior to her death. She was in a facility that specialized in memory care and was assigned to a tiny room with a roommate. Her appetite was poor, so I had stopped for apple pies from a fast food chain. At this point, I thought she should eat whatever she wanted, so I was catering to her sweet tooth. We visited in her room and ate our pies while she told me tons of stories about her life. She talked about being electrocuted in the cow barn at age thirteen and how the jolt threw her off the milking stool and against the back wall. After this, the magnetic field in her body was messed up, and she couldn't keep charge in a watch battery. A new one would die in about a day, and it got too expensive. I researched and found that this isn't too uncommon. That's why wind-up watches are still man-ufactured today. Grandma talked about how the love of her life was still Grandpa Francis and that he broke her heart. She told me even though she and my dad consistently gave each other a hard time, she really respected him. When she looked into my eyes, I knew she was still my sweet Grandma. She held my hand and told me, "Whatever you do, never stop going to church." Grandma loved the Lord, and she always advised that if there was trouble in your life, you should pray about it.

We talked about the summer I turned ten, and I got to stay for a whole week at her farm. I had the time of my life. We picked strawberries, snapped green beans, and went for walks all over her property. She showed me how to collect eggs from the chickens, and that became my job for the week. There was no one like my Grandma. When I accepted Christ at age thirteen, I remember her sweetly saying, "Welcome to the family." Then she gave me a big hug, and we all sat in church together. At her memorial service, the pastor read a letter she had written to him from her assisted living facility. She wrote that she was keeping his family and ministry in her prayers. Ella was a woman of incredible faith and never ever stopped trusting in the power of prayer.

My grandmother's passing was terribly bittersweet. The progression of a disease in the mind was difficult to watch. She faded away quickily. She went from being the caretaker to being the one taken care of. As she and my mother exchanged roles, I tried to be there for support. Grandma would no longer be the giver of advice or a pillar of strength, and she would leave us a long time before her body was ready to go. The very last time I saw her, I met my mother at the nursing home. There was no conversation, no recognition, and no attempt at connection. There were only infantile moans of discomfort. We held her hand and smoothed the hair on her brow to quiet her into sleep. A few days later, she left us for heaven, a place where all things are made new. Praise Jesus!

# The Advocate

As women, we wear a lot of hats throughout our lives. Through the years our roles change, as does our circle of influence. The role of *advocate* is one of the most important roles we will ever play, however. Through good times and difficult ones, we are not alone in our struggle to do the right thing at the right time in all situations.

I think our first opportunity to advocate comes with the birth of our first child. We get to know that child and learn that every little sound or cry has a particular meaning. We know the difference between the cry of hunger and the cry of discomfort—even the fake cry of boredom. Sometimes we'll seek assistance just because our gut is telling us something isn't quite right, though we may have no clue what it is. Experience will guide us in caring for our children, and eventually, we learn as mothers what requires real worry and real action. Folks often joke that children of nurses have it worst of all, insisting that there has to be actual blood loss or a projecting bone before we head for medical care. That's a bit exaggerated, but we do know from our work experience what really constitutes a medical emergency.

As kids enter school, it takes time for us to develop a trust in the school system. We're on the watch for delays in learning, especially if that type of thing runs in your family. I remember particularly struggling to advocate for my daughter during her kindergarten and first-grade years. She had demonstrated a difficulty in concentration and an inability to perform tasks she had been given. Our friend watched her after school on days that I had to work and brought to my attention that she had to practically sit on her to get spelling words written five times. What my friend shared with me sounded all too familiar. Our daughter could be instructed to go upstairs to change her clothes and would find ninety other things to do along the way. I would often find her clothes only half changed, playing with a doll and watching TV, instead of heading back downstairs for Sunday dinner. I learned early on to give her about ten minutes and then go check on her to remind her of my instructions. My brother had had similar issues and was finally diagnosed at age seventeen with ADHD. Getting the process started was difficult, but I was determined to get my daughter the help she needed, and eventually I was successful. Laina was tested after we moved to North Dakota, and then after speaking with our physician (and teachers) she was started on medication and a 504 plan. For the next few years, the school would place an extra teacher in the classroom, primarily to assist Laina with paying attention and staying on task. Establishing all of this took most of her first-grade year and lots of conversations, appointments, and meetings. It was stressful but necessary, and I knew in my heart that I was doing the right thing for my child. If she was to have a normal life without the struggle I watched my brother face, I had to advocate as early as possible.

Moving from Alaska to North Dakota was terribly disruptive, but that's how it goes in the military world. Reestablishing our network of support with physicians, teachers, and later, a therapist would take time. The move came right in the midst of making headway in treatment for the ADHD. In the meantime, I was reading books about the subject, educating myself on dietary changes we could make to give her an advantage. We opted for high-protein breakfasts, tried to avoid sugar, and kept her medications on time. At this point, Laina took a pill in the morning and one at noon, which the school nurse administered. By middle school, the stigma of going to the office for medicine drew too much attention from her peers. Kids are insensitive and ask prying personal questions. In general, they are cruel. We had the medication changed to once daily so that there was no need for the extra attention of the pill at noon. As she entered high school, medications were completely stopped, but therapy continued to help as we struggled to maintain a household routine that worked for all of us. We were given memory games to help Laina remember tasks and lots of support and ideas for accommodation. Making lists, wearing a watch, and keeping a day planner are all things we utilized. Laina kept her 504 plan through twelve years of school and found that in college, she did not need accommodation. Methods of coping and accommodating for the short attention span have been incredibly helpful.

At this point, the story sounds pretty smooth. Unfortunately, the move to Illinois after Bryan's military retirement would shake things up again. In an attempt to minimize the stress of moving, we strategically planned to move between eighth grade and high school. This transition was going to be rough anyway, so we felt it was the best time to do it. Transplanting into a small town with a consolidated school proved tougher than we thought. About nine months after our move, Bryan's dad suddenly passed away from a heart attack, devastating Laina more than any of the rest of us. Laina continued to be bullied by others, and social media was no help in the matter. Anyone who had it in for her now had twenty-four-hour access, which I hated and tried to prevent. I don't think I let the kids use social media until they were thirteen for this very reason. The ADHD would continue to affect absolutely every type of relationship she had. It makes friendships, dating, and parenting very tough. A little research taught me that ADHD kids fall behind their peers an average of two to three years in anything involving eye-hand coordination, making many tasks difficult. This explains why tying shoes or riding a bike came so late for her years ago, and why she wasn't ready to drive until she turned eighteen. Looking back, giving her space and time was the best thing we did. Once again, I was advocating.

Laina was a girl full of talent. She inherited my musical ability and was involved in choir and theater as early as I can recall. She often played starring roles in musicals and was madrigal queen her senior year of high school. Laina found her niche in music, but it took a lot of soul searching to figure out what she might do for a career. Technical training is often more appropriate for individuals with ADHD, and so in the end, she chose to major in culinary studies, which her father and I totally supported. In retrospect, Laina has spent more time in the kitchen than anyone else I know. Throughout her childhood, it was necessary to keep her within arm's length from me while I cooked supper each night. Staying focused on her homework after medications had worn off was difficult. What worked best for us was doing homework in the kitchen while I cooked. Thus, a love for cooking was born.

Like any teen, we faced issues, both emotional and social. Depression after the loss of her grandfather, compiled with her first high school break-up brought her to a new low. We nearly lost our dog a month after this due to bladder stones, and the blows kept coming. The year Laina was seventeen was probably the worst year ever. I didn't know who she was, and I don't think she did, either. This particular year brought trouble and fear and a low point like I have never experienced as a parent. Simultaneously, we still hadn't found a church home in Illinois. Laina needed a church family as much as she needed her real family. This kind of support is crucial in surviving the teen years. Lucky for us, therapy was helpful, and some friendships developed, which led to eventually finding a church home for our family. All of this happened in God's time and not in mine. My job as her mother was to put her in God's protective arms every day and trust that He alone could even protect her from self-harm. I continued to advocate.

As a young adult, I see so many wonderful and positive changes in my daughter. I've seen her develop coping skills that I wish I had myself. She is so gifted in her enthusiasm for cooking and will graduate from a local culinary program in about a month or so. She has a boyfriend, and he seems very supportive. She still lives at home at this point in time. God has placed her in the most perfect situation for a first job after college: she is the head cook for our local Christian service camp. What a great way to serve and what a great atmosphere to work in! I continue to pray for her success and for God to use her to her fullest capacity through this new job. As she spreads her wings and branches out beyond this first job, I pray that every step she takes will be blessed. I pray that everyone she comes in contact with will be a blessing to her and that her life will

be an example of how very good our God truly is. As her mother, I

will never stop advocating.

# The Art of Letting Go

As a mother of two children, I do my best to keep our life balanced. Navigating the teenage years has been just as tricky as raising babies. There's a fine balance between how much space to give them and how much to hover. You wonder if you are doing the right thing and giving the right advice. Factoring in their many moods, your stress level, and possible sleep deprivation, and an encounter with your child can go either super great or very badly. When they share personal details, you don't want to seem judgmental because if you damage the relationship they'll get advice from someone else. The only way to ensure the best possible outcome is to rely on God in every way. Remember that there is no such thing as a perfect family. But, if you let God guide you in all areas of your life, including parenting, you can ensure the best possible outcome. Also, remember that the desired outcome is to raise a fully-functioning adult who can support themselves and leaves home to spread their wings and fly. I wonder if Mary and Joseph had half the melt-down I've had when Jesus left home to start his ministry. Fortunately, they knew they were raising the son of God, and at the age of twelve, He was fully aware of who He was and why He was sent to earth. Was Mary nervous when she hadn't heard from Jesus in a week or so? Did she worry that the twelve apostles would somehow be a bad influence? The Bible doesn't really talk about their family dynamics in detail, but Mary and Joseph were parents, and I imagine they experienced lots of routine normal emotions when their son left home. What was it like for Jesus? Was He just totally filled with the excitement of ministry, or did He ever get homesick?

There are two sides to this growing-up business. For a moment, let's remember what it was like to be the young adult leaving home. In all honesty, there is no way to leave home without it being abrupt. And, whether it happens when you leave for college or when you finally marry, everyone rips that bandage off. You're torn between this thing you want (separating from your parents and being a part of a new family unit) and staying where you've been comfortable and supported for years. The nervousness and anticipation definitely come with the territory. As described in elsewhere in this book, I lived at home with my parents all through college and commuted across town to class. There's a part of me that wonders if living on campus would have been helpful or if it would have been a distraction. Maybe living apart from my parents before I got married would have been good for me. At the time, it seemed pointless to pay more to live in a different space. So, my college experience was whatever I needed at the time. If I had a reason to stay on campus, I found friends and classmates to hang out with. When I'd had enough of it, I retreated home to those four walls where I felt safe and unconditionally loved. That's the primary reason why I didn't leave home to attend nursing school. I would have been terribly homesick.

I promised my mother that I would have my college education completed before I married. My parents had met in Bible college and married shortly after they met. My mom quit school and went to work while my dad finished his degree to become a pastor. This was common practice in the 1970s. Since my mom didn't get to finish college (and had an early dream to go into nursing) my completion of school was extremely imperative. It was very important to her that I fulfil my goal, so I assured her that I would have graduation guaranteed before I got married. Spring break of 1994, Bryan and I exchanged vows during a small ceremony at my parent's home. My dad officiated, my brother gave me away, and our mothers cried. The event was small and private but beautiful, and my dad was sweating bullets! I don't have many pictures of that day, and I believe our mothers were using 110 cameras at that time. My favorite photo is the one of us cutting the cake. It turned out better than any of the other pictures (I'm also a huge fan of cake, so there's a real sense of enthusiasm on my face). Looking at pictures from that day, Bryan and I look like babies. Bryan was twenty-two, and I was twenty-one, and we were so in love. All we wanted was to take this huge leap together. The weekend of my graduation from college, my parents threw us a big reception at our church, and both sides of the family were invited. We celebrated the wedding and my BSN degree at the same time, giving us all an opportunity to connect before I moved away to a new life.

We drove down to Little Rock where Bryan was stationed and stayed together in our little off-base apartment for our honeymoon.

I enjoyed decorating and setting up our new place together. I still had two months of school to finish, so I continued living with my parents, and Bryan commuted six hours every weekend until I was graduated. The morning after graduation, we packed up our car and my in-law's truck with everything I had accumulated to move and drove down to Arkansas. Halfway there, I lost all composure and fell apart. "I don't think I can do this," I said, as I sobbed into my hands. Bryan pulled the car over and said, "Yes, you can. I'm right here." Then he told me about when he left for boot camp with the Air Force. He shared about how upset he was during his first night away from home and how he wasn't allowed to call them at all during his training. That bandage was ripped off quickly.

I think I called my mom twice a day for a couple of weeks until I got busy with the daily tasks of regular life. I was a mess on the phone, but my mom seemed totally fine, which I couldn't understand. Somehow, she managed to hide her emotions from me and seemed so incredibly strong. She said it was nice to have me around for those four extra years, to have help with the house, adult conversations, and to watch me mature in my faith. I was getting ready for adult life, and there were a lot of changes going on. I look back now and wonder if I'm doing well at handling my own children growing up and moving away. As we discuss my son's pending high school graduation, his fall class schedule for community college, and his ultimate career goals, I try to keep my composure. Just last week, we had this very mature conversation, and I didn't get upset until thirty minutes afterward. I went outside to work on a project with Bryan and just began weeping. Once again I said, "I don't think I can do this." And once again, he told me, "Yes, you can. I'm right here." Nearly thirty years later, my dad shared with me that my mom cried for about two weeks straight after I moved away. I'd better stock up on tissues.

In truth, from the moment our children are born, we practice the art of letting go. That first week, it's hard to put them in anyone else's hands. Dropping them off for forty-five minutes in the church nursery can be traumatic for a new mother. It's sometimes months before we feel we can go out for a date with our spouse and leave the baby with a sitter. And, the whole time we're out, the conversation will generally be about the baby. We get nervous, so we'll make a call to check on the baby, unsure if we've done the right thing by leaving them with someone. You'll be certain that if you die today, it'll be from guilt. (It's totally natural and completely nuts!) You will get better at this, but it isn't easy. Over the course of eighteen years, there will be tons of opportunity to practice letting go—daycare, babysitters, putting them on a school bus (the first day of school was always a *total* weep fest), and then watching them drive away in a car, but don't get me started on the car issue. You'll watch as they develop friendships and relationships and face both joy and disappointment. You'll be at every ballgame and school play, not only to share in their success, but to be the first responder if things don't go right. Christian moms learn to pray for protection if their child is more than twenty feet away from them, and they never stop praying. Probably the best piece of advice I ever received was from a co-worker. We were discussing kids leaving for college and how to know that they make good choices. She reminded me of the scripture about "training a child the way he should go and when he is old he will not depart from it" (Proverbs 22:6). I know this scripture, and it's brought me calm many times. She also reminded me to pray for every person my child will come in contact with and that they would be the right kind of influences. I will need to do this daily for my own sanity.

The greater truth to be learned through all of this is that praying for our children is the most important thing we can do for them. When they are further than our arms can reach, they should be wrapped in prayer. Our heavenly Father promised that He would "never leave us or forsake us" (Deuteronomy 31:6) and that He would "be with you until the very end of the age" (Matthew 28:20). You can be assured that this promise is true and lasting. It can give us a real sense of peace when we experience that terrible separation anxiety (trust me; it isn't just the children who face it). Knowing that when your child cannot be in your arms, he or she is in God's arms. Isn't He the best example of parenting that we have? Keeping lines of communication open is also important. You want your adult child to feel they can come to you with any issue they face. This presents the wonderful opportunity for you all to pray together for problems and concerns. Decision-making can be hard, so not only does your child need to benefit from your advice and experience, but you can demonstrate the practice of seeking help from God. In the end we're really not letting go. We're letting God do what He does best.

# The Grace of Exhortation

A patient of mine once told me that from the moment he met me, he knew my spiritual gift was that of exhortation. More simply stated, I have the gift of encouraging others. And, from the moment I met him, he required much encouragement. As a nurse of twenty-three years, my current job is in a long-term acute care facility. More specifically, we take care of patients who have large wounds to be healed, need to be weaned off of ventilators (and have tracheostomies), or require IV antibiotics for several weeks to fight infections. The average length of stay is thirty days. I've taken care of a lot of people in various situations, and John's story (I've changed his name to protect his identity) was strikingly similar to many others in that he was transferred to my hospital for lengthy antibiotic therapy. The most memorable thing about his arrival was how much pain he was in, and my immediate goal was to get that pain under control. Once the pain was controlled, we could go about the business of settling John into this new setting and explaining the routines and the care he would be receiving. His wife and daughter arrived soon after he did, and I could tell they were anxious to see what things would be like for him there. I briefly explained what I could about our facility and what they could expect over the coming days. Unfortunately, my shift ended, and another nurse completed the rest of John's admission.

I had a few days off from work and was assigned to care for John again the next week. Over the days that followed, we would have discussions about his condition and his slow but steady improvement. Because I hadn't seen him every single day, I could better appreciate his progress. I noticed his increase in activity, reduction in pain, and healing of wounds, and I encouraged him. My advice to John was that slow, steady improvement was far better than a big jump forward and then a setback. He agreed. He was working with physical therapy and gaining ground each and every day. He went from being totally bedfast to spending his day in a recliner with his feet up, and eventually he had permission to get up alone with a walker to go to the bathroom. All of this was excellent. Still, to maintain a positive outlook, I continued to share what I could see from my vantage point as his nurse. From one day to the next, there might not have been an impressive reduction in his need for pain medications or improvement in his mobility; however, after a couple of days off and then returning, he seemed to be improving tremendously. One thing I noticed about John is that he maintained a certain level of joy no matter what was going on, so long as I continued to share my perspective with him.

John was in his mid-seventies, and I learned from our nurse practitioner that he was a pastor. Not only that, but he was a pastor's kid (I'm also a pastor's kid). Knowing this about him opened up an entirely new area of conversation between us. We had more in common than I originally thought, and while I performed his dressing changes or carried out other tasks for him, we talked about so many things. John not only pastored but has been a counselor for years. I enjoyed our visits not only because it made him more joyful, but because he turned things around and shared his perspective with me on many topics. He reminded me a lot of my dad, who always gives me a biblical answer prior to giving me his opinion on anything. Eventually, I mentioned to him that I had been working on writing a book. His eyes seriously lit up when I told him. He asked me all kinds of things about it and shared with me that he had helped his secretary with a book in the past few years and how much he enjoyed that process. I tried to explain the style of my book and the audience I hoped to reach with it. He was excited to see what I had done with it and agreed to take a brief look and give me his opinion. I have to say that I was incredibly nervous to hand John those pages to read. He was the first nonfamily member to read any portion of it, and there was potential for me to become very disappointed in the work as a whole. I tried to select a few of my favorite chapters for him to read, hoping John would be impressed while bracing myself for criticism. I had both feelings of nervous excitement and also dread. As I placed those pages in his hands, I felt as if I were handing him my firstborn child to guard and protect, silly as that sounds. Luckily, the shift was especially busy, and I was soon too distracted by other tasks to worry much about it.

After a few hours, John put on his call light and asked for me to come discuss the portions of the book he had read. I honestly needed this, but I was incredibly nervous. Feedback from someone who barely knew me was the best thing in the world. I sat down briefly while John gave me honest and true advice. He was kind and never said the book was awful; he simply stated that it was incredibly factual and since it detailed portions of my life and my testimony, facts are great. What he said to me is that if the book was to appeal to total strangers around the globe (and if it was to be helpful to folks in similar situations to the ones I describe), I needed to expand. I needed to write in such a way that people who don't know me at all would understand and come to know me. Better yet, they would come to know the God who carried me through those tough situations. Unlike more popular Christian writers who already have a voice (and are well-known), I don't have a voice yet. The key was expansion. John said I should take each individual chapter and give them to God and have Him help me to expand them. I sat there, hoping that I didn't look like I was angry or about to cry. Initially, it took everything I had to not appear my feelings were hurt at John's comments. I had placed myself in a very vulnerable position in asking for his advice on the book. He realized this, and he delivered his criticism with as much grace as one can imagine. He praised me for my willingness to share the sometimes difficult experiences of my life in the hopes of helping others but said there had to be something to pique their interest and keep them reading.

I couldn't have asked for better advice. As hard as it was to hear, it was important to me to get an honest opinion from someone who knew what they were talking about. John had helped write and edit books in the past, and there was so much value in his counsel. He was also a man who let God direct his life, and he became the perfect person to give me an honest opinion. He delivered his criticism in such a way that I wasn't completely crushed. Much to my surprise, I found myself psyched-up to meet his challenge of expansion. For the rest of the shift, when I entered John's room to take him medication or do his dressing changes, he could tell the wheels of creativity were turning. I wasn't in a position to sit down and fix those chapters immediately, but the process of how to fix them was already brewing in my mind. Before I left for the day, I thanked John for his willingness to take part in the making of what I hope will be an incredibly inspiring work.

Everything happens for a reason and in God's timing. The people we encounter who bring a blessing to our lives may vanish just as quickly as they showed up. God knows our need and sends someone to meet that need. Philippians 4:19 says that "God shall supply all your needs according to his riches in glory through Christ Jesus." We simply have to lay our needs at the feet of Jesus daily in prayer. No matter how big or small our request is He orchestrates this beautiful tapestry of human interaction in a way that utilizes those who are willing to be His hands and His feet. John has legitimate physical needs that I am meeting through my job as a nurse. I administer his medications, maintain his safety, and perform his dressing changes so that healing can take place. John has met my need as a nurse to find fulfillment in my job. He prays for me, encourages me with my book writing, and appreciates the tasks I perform. He's even laid hands on my painful elbow and prayed that I would be delivered from tendonitis and discomfort. John showed up at a time when I was feeling very burned out as a nurse and unappreciated. Because of the friendship we've developed, I really feel more joyful. Taking care of John helps to balance out the difficult personalities I deal with at my job, and he's been like a breath of fresh air! I am confident that God sent him to renew my love for what I'm called to do. I'll continue to use my gift of exhortation at every opportunity and allow God to encourage others through me.

After all, it's about expansion.

# It'll All Come out in the Wash

I try not to define my life by one single moment, be it good or bad, but to allow all the events on my timeline to be pages in the book about my life. On occasion, I get a little stuck, though. I'm stuck on a page that is uncomfortable and emotional, and it seems to flavor every moment of every day. Maybe you have felt this way, too? The season I'm in is traditionally a positive and happy time for people. Graduations are such wonderful celebrations! This past spring, we celebrated two: Our daughter graduated from a culinary program and our son from high school. So I have children who are nearly grown, and my first one is moving away from the family nest. The younger of the two is about to enter college, and although he's living at home for the next two years, he's still reached a milestone which my heart recognizes as "leaving."

My head knows that we've been preparing for these events since the day the kids were born. My heart, however, is protesting in unpredictable ways like I have never known. Part of me honestly thought I must be entering menopause or something because I've been bursting into tears at the drop of a hat. I'm not sleeping well. The last time I was part of this type of situation I was, in fact, the one leaving. I had packed my things and was heading down south with my new husband to start our life together. When you're the one leaving, the perspective is totally different. You're headed *toward* something new and wonderful. I was both scared and excited at the same time. This side of the fence feels a lot different, and I'm not sure I like it. This time, I'm the anxious parent left watching while that car pulls out of the driveway. Being left behind to worry about the kind of people my grown children will encounter feels a lot like when they rode the school bus for the first time. It's terrible. While I'm excited for my daughter's adventures of her first apartment and first real job, there's a part of me that feels abandoned or no longer needed. It's irrational, I know. But, it's the best way I can describe it.

I can still remember the day I called my mom and was upset over the terrible twos. Laina was two, and the only word I'd used all day was "no." I put her down for an afternoon nap and got out a Christian parenting book that we'd received as a baby shower gift. I remember as I read the chapter on toddlerhood, asking my mother, "At what point does this process ever become fun?" I'm pretty sure she laughed. Every age and stage brought with it joy and anxiety, which is normal. You keep your eye on the desired end result, which is raising well-rounded, kind, godly kids who grow up and eventually follow their own path in life. The rest of the messy daily stuff has to just roll off. It's been a long time since toddlerhood, but it's as fresh in my mind as yesterday. I admit that along the way there were learning curves. I learned that discipline is necessary if I really love my child. After all, "The Lord disciplines the ones He loves, and He chastens everyone He accepts as his son" (Hebrews 12:6). I kept the kids in church through the years (even if we went without their dad) and did my best to provide a godly upbringing. Every age and stage with my children has been enjoyable, and now as adults, we have a close relationship with them.

I was proud of myself for keeping my composure and not crying during Brandon's high school graduation ceremony. It helped that there was video footage of him clowning around, and it really broke the tension. Then there was the party we threw for him with friends and family afterward. Between food preparation and visiting with guests, there wasn't time to fall apart. There were lots of distractions. I was mostly okay until the day we went out to pay his first semester tuition and then went to lunch (once the money is paid, it's officially happening). Later that evening, I broke down. He and I have entered a new phase, and now he will learn more about responsibility and respect than he has ever known in his life. I believe we've helped to shape a wonderful young man, and he's in God's hands every time he walks out my front door.

Add to my emotional stress, the stress of a physical injury. I've literally been dealing with arm pain for months. I slipped on an icy sidewalk and landed on my elbow last December. Everything seemed to be okay until February when I had a large patient almost fall out of bed and I managed to injure my arm again. As a nurse, I have seen people in chronic pain become depressed and despondent. I always advise them that healing takes time, and some processes cannot be rushed. I remind them to ask for help if they need it and to not feel guilty about getting the rest they need. Why is it that I cannot take my own advice and extend this grace to myself? Just brushing my hair is painful, so I took steps to find out what's really wrong. Today I had an MRI. Surgery might even be required to get me back to normal. If that takes place, I will follow the physician's instructions, attend therapy, and face the reality that a physical nursing job may not be appropriate for me anymore. I'm supposed to be covering for a co-worker's maternity leave in a different capacity than my normal job title, and there may not be time to train me. So far, I haven't been issued the tools needed to successfully cover for her. I'm beginning to wonder if agreeing to cover her leave was the right thing to do in the first place. If surgery is necessary, then I won't be doing either of those jobs. Time off from work to recover isn't going to help the family budget. This feels like such a mess! And so, the stress begins.

I'm sure there are situations in all of our lives where we feel pushed to the wall, and we wonder which way is up. Our heads can be spinning from feeling constantly bombarded with stresses from every direction. We've done the math, and the numbers just don't add up. The path we're on may seem confusing, and based upon our own understanding, we can't see how our very messy lives are going to work out okay. Thankfully, God sees our beautiful messes and is there to help us carry the load. We don't have to tidy anything up for Him to fix things. The daily struggles that we face and the victories we experience are all orchestrated by a wonderful, loving God. He allows us to feel joy, sorrow, grief, and contentment, and He holds the world in the very palm of His hand. He cares about the smallest of details, and He asks that we cast all of our anxieties on Him because he cares for us (1 Peter 5:7). The troubles we face are important to Him because He will demonstrate his power and grace by the way in which He brings us through them. Each one of those becomes part of our personal testimony and brings God glory and honor like nothing else can. When our situation seems most impossible is when He does his very best work.

So, I give to God my parenting (which will continue because my kids will always need me). My worries about Brandon attending college and Laina moving out, I also give to Him. I'll let Him handle my work stress and the fear I have about my physical injury. God can handle my financial concerns and all the things that keep me up at night. I'll give him my marriage because He is the glue that keeps my husband and me together. Prayer is the number one remedy for all that stresses us, and if a person were to say a little prayer each and every time a troubled thought entered their minds, that person might be talking to God all day long. That is not to say that you have to lock yourself away in a private place all day until you get the answer to your prayer because that's not productive, but you might just say a little silent prayer in your head while you drive to work or while you walk to a meeting. You can even pray while you clean. Praying without ceasing was an instruction in the Bible and is completely timeless and effective (1 Thessalonians 5:17). You'll feel dramatically lighter when you let God carry the load of your burdens and cares. You have absolutely nothing to lose, except stress.

# Journaling Faith

## Day 1

We all know people who seem to have it all together. Maybe, on occasion, we actually give the impression that we have the entire "God" thing figured out. When you're in an unfamiliar setting or you don't know people very well, they don't appear stressed. They make it look easy. They seem comfortable in their walk of faith, and their lives appear to be struggle-free. It could be that they, like you, put their best foot forward on Sundays. They go through the motions of the worship service, unaffected, *while I'm wiping tears away during the communion meditation.* I've come to realize that there is a degree of brokenness in every single person sitting in the service with me. It's the degree of vulnerability or sensitivity that creates those moments where God literally reaches into your soul and pulls out the hurt. I'm not tearful every Sunday, but there have been many times when the words to a song will strike a cord and touch my heart very deeply. When we are weak, God strengthens us, and when we are broken, He fills us. It's totally okay to be that person who doesn't have it all together or all worked out. Our entire lives are the process by which God refines us and molds us, perfecting our faith and drawing us ever closer to Him. Today I brought God my awful mess and laid it all out there for Him to examine.

My week has been full of prayer time. Potential job loss due to injury and other factors has me on my knees like never before. This isn't just one of those platitudes where I'm speaking loosely of prayer in a theoretical way. This is me being terribly real. Talking the talk means walking the walk. This past week I was sent home from work and immediately started losing hours. The decision to honor my second round of light duty has to come from much higher in our company. Someone at the corporate level has to decide if I'm allowed to work my hours with no lifting and potential tendon surgery in the very near future. It's become very complicated. I came to the conclusion that from this point on, we need to be frugal as if I'm unemployed and concentrate on God meeting our needs. I pray that He will help me discern between needs and wants and that our family will be sustained. I've started my days this week with coffee and my prayer notebook. I quickly sit and make a list of all the things to pray about and also the praises to thank Him for. Once I'm happy with the list, I get down on my knees and lower my head to the floor right over that list and I pray about every single item. Sometimes I only pray once, and other days I pray a second time. If I'm especially anxious about anything in particular, I say a little prayer in my head while I go about my housework. It's actually calming to just give God every little anxiety.

Thursday, we had an answer to prayer in that Bryan now has approval and an appointment for an MRI on his knee, which he injured at work. This is a big praise on my list because he's been waiting for several weeks and has been in pain. I'll continue to pray for surgery if needed and for God's will in this situation.

Today's church service was especially meaningful. The songs we sang and the message that the pastor presented were tai-lor-made for my situation. All the scriptures were like statements of hope directly from God just for me. Small groups will be starting up soon, and one of the things I've been specifically praying for is that Bryan and I would be able to join one this fall as a couple. I've attended a few rounds of small group in a female-only setting, but it was really nice a few years ago when we were both going to a group together. Anyway, a woman approached us with a jam jar to return. Laina had worked all summer at the church camp with her daughter, and this woman knew and liked Laina very much. She had hosted the camp workers at her house for a couple of events and had gotten to know her. Laina had given her friend's mother a jar of my jam. It turns out that this woman was in a Bible study with me a couple of years ago, and thanks to social media, she came to realize the connection between me and Laina. Anyway, she and her husband host a small group, and they don't mind if you attend occasionally. I had been praying that a group would surface that we could join, and without warning, the group invitation came right to me! I think this was God's way of helping me find the right group. This is what I choose to believe. I left for home with a feeling that God will honor all His promises to take care of my family and meet our needs. He's already starting to do amazing things.

## Day 2

9 a.m.: I woke up this morning to a phone call from my payroll department at work. The gal on the phone needed my permission to supplement the hours I didn't get, working with vacationhours. I, of course, gave her permission to use them and immediately my mind is flooded with anxiety about how many vacation hours I have left and how long it will last. I washed my face, brushed my teeth, and headed downstairs to make a cup of coffee and jot down this morning's prayer list. Without hesitation, I was on my knees, thanking God for the blessings of yesterday. I thanked Him for the potential small group leaders' invitation, for all the free supplies we received for our garden project (free mulch for a garden covering), and for a wonderful weekend with Laina home to help me. Yesterday's sermon seemed to be tailored for exactly what I'm going through, and even the songs on my radio station were speaking directly to my specific needs. Yesterday was full of blessings straight from God, and I need to operate today in total trust and with a thankful heart for all of those things.

I have to share that in the midst of what I'm calling "turmoil," there is an incredible sense of peace for me. There's a really great painting that I saw once at the Christian bookstore, prior to their unfortunate nationwide closure. It was a painting of a deep blue, roaring sea with waves like something you'd see in a movie. The painter did a phenomenal job of capturing the motion of wind and waves, making them appear dangerous and ominous, I imagine that if the weather called for seas like this, you'd better stay home and not be caught up in the dangerous swells. Yet, in the very center of this painting stands a lighthouse and in the doorway of the light-house stands a man who is ever-so-casually leaning against the doorframe. He doesn't appear distressed, and he isn't hanging on for dear life. He seems strangely peaceful, amidst monster waves that keep crashing against the lighthouse walls. So, despite how the potentially deep waves of turmoil attempt to swallow me, I'm safe in the peaceful doorway of God's lighthouse right now. I'm taking each and every stress to Him because He promised the "peace which passes all understanding" (Philippians 4:7). I now have an appoint-ment tomorrow to speak with someone at work about the possibility of being able to work at all, and ordinarily this would make me really edgy and upset, but I'm not. God's got this!

## Day 3

Noon: I had a meeting with our human resources director this morning, and she didn't say anything I hadn't already imagined she'd say. We had a very calm and civilized conversation about the situation of my injury and my physician's recommendations. While I try to be positive for others, for myself, the glass is half-empty at times. I imagined the worst-case scenario, which is that they would tell me I have to go on some type of disability and cannot accrue any active shifts. At this time, they will not honor any request for job modification or light duty, so I am stuck. I'm imagining the man in my lighthouse painting, standing in the doorway and becoming slightly frazzled because he's getting wet with spray from the ocean waves. The waves are wild and even though he's relatively safe from danger, those waters won't be ignored. Getting wet is far better than being carried away by torrid seas. The man in the painting is safe but still affected by the presence of the crazy ocean. I called my husband and my mother, both amazingly supportive people. But it's time to pray again before the salt water stings my eyes.

4 p.m.: There's a lot to process. I go back and forth between a state of complete trust in God to meet my needs and a horrible

state of anxiety. This feeling of helplessness is terrible. I'm okay when Bryan's here and we can calmly talk or pray together, but I'm an emotional mess when I'm alone for too long. I suppose because I'm human, this state of flux between the two is normal, and this is where the real struggle lies. I'm caught up in the fear of what tomorrow holds, and while my heart knows that God has the whole world in the palm of His hand, my head is realistically looking at our pile of monthly bills and wondering how we'll manage. Putting faith into action calls for huge amounts of prayer, so that's my plan for right now, and I'll keep the journal updated.

## Day 4

I probably failed to mention this, but I do photography as a hobby. Up to this point, I've done florals, landscapes, and senior pictures for family and friends. I have a supply of printed note cards from a couple of years ago that could be lucrative if I have the right setting for a sale. I've never been one to sit at a festival booth and market this stuff, but I have contacted a couple of shops downtown, which feature art from local artisans. They deal with jewelry and pottery but sometimes paintings and photographs. I did hear back from one of them last night, and then I forwarded them pictures of my work. Once they decide if it's something they're interested in, I could have an outlet for marketing some photographs. How exciting is that? I also made a poster for the post office communication board, letting folks know that I exist and that they can contact me for pictures. In a tiny town like mine, you see all sorts of ads for babysitting or yard-work. Maybe some work will come my way, and we'll be blessed with some additional income. I'm praying that God will bless these efforts, and my phone will ring with folks needing "pictures at an incredible value." I would love to be very busy taking pictures.

2 p.m.: today I reached out to an old friend from North Dakota. She was a part of our women's group at Thrive Community Church, and she is a fierce prayer warrior. Hearing her response to my e-mail was like a breath of fresh air. *Seriously*. And I know that no matter how long it's been since we've spoken, friends in God are *amazing*! She brought her unique insight and humor into my very serious situation and will be praying with and for us through this process that God is bringing us through. She reminded me that all hard times are like storms in the ocean and that there is no storm that doesn't know God's name. He can calm any storm, and while

it's raging on and on, He often calms the ones in the middle of it. God is incredibly good.

## Day 5

Okay, so several days have passed including a long, holiday weekend. There have been emotional ups and downs for me as I navigate this uncomfortable season in my life. Overall, I felt that I experienced God's blessings through a phone call from a work friend and a great day at church this past Sunday, but the weekend was peppered with dismal moments in which I felt helpless and discouraged. I'm pretty sure this is normal. It can be so difficult to maintain a positive attitude when the realist in you is freaking out at the possibility that a financial wrecking ball is headed your way. Occasionally, I just experience a moment of sheer panic, and it's during those times that I stop and pray until it passes. I will tell you, though, that prayers are already being answered in awesome ways. Bryan was approached by another man after church in regard to a group that does target shooting and fellowship. God sent someone to invite him to be a part of a group of Christian men, which may provide a way for him to be more involved. Between our invitation to join a small group and this invitation, God is providing fellowship opportunities, which is a great way to find support and to bless others at the same time. God is amazing.

## Day 6

Today I feel blessed. I started my day with my first cup of coffee and then my prayer time. I find that when I focus on God first, the day doesn't fall apart. Then I headed out to the post office, which is only four blocks from my house. It was a cool fall morning, and the sun was shining. A neighbor a few doors down was doing yardwork and paused both on my way to and from the post office to wish me a good morning and then to remark about how nice the day is. He's a retired gentleman, and up until this point, I don't believe we've ever spoken. I reentered my house to be welcomed by the aroma of coffee, which always makes me happy. To me, there's just something about the smell of brewing coffee that's so welcoming and uplifting. After a quick shower, I opened up the windows on the main floor of the house and was inspired to write this morning about how absolutely glorious the day is going to be. I'm focused on my blessings instead of my fears, and I'm embracing the reality that God is in control of my life. I believe that He is going to do a mighty work in my life and in the life of my family. These things will be a testimony to His goodness. This morning I am confident that the God I serve will provide for our needs "according to His riches in glory" (Philippians 4:19).

I've described feelings of hopelessness that I occasionally have. It's totally human nature to occasionally doubt. After all, our parents raise us to be independent, and totally trusting God goes completely against the natural tendency to handle things in our own way and by ourselves. I drift up and down what I describe as a "continuum of faith." It's kind of like the pain scale that nurses might use to have a patient describe their level of pain. Generally, it's a scale from zero to ten in which zero indicates absolutely no pain, and ten is the worst pain imaginable. I would place nonbelievers at the zero and those who have totally given their lives to Christ at ten. Somewhere along the scale would be the different levels of belief, and let's say for argument's sake that we put a newly baptized believer at a five on the scale. A new Christian believes in Christ and has accepted Him as their savior, but now they have to continue to grow and develop that faith. I would say that the average active Christian travels up and down the scale somewhere between the five and the ten on almost a daily basis. It doesn't mean we're weak or that we don't trust God totally. The purpose of the continuum is to account for the times that the world attempts to sway us or influence us. Between technology, constant social media, and our own tendency for self-preservation, the level we maintain is dependent on how much time we spend in prayer, Bible study, and with other Christians. I do know of a woman whose husband began their marriage many years ago, at a good solid eight. He served as a deacon in their church, and they raised their children in church. Not long after the children were grown and gone, he announced to her that he wasn't sure he even believed there was a God. It's totally possible to go from ten to zero, which saddens me greatly. My hope and prayer is that any of us who declare Christ as Lord will work to maintain that closeness with Him. Maintaining a fellowship with other believers as we are called to do "do not forsake the fellowship," (Hebrews 10:25) and look for ways to serve others.

So, today I feel like I'm a good, solid nine on that continuum of faith scale. That is not to say that anxiety might not set in at some point in the day. But, when it does, I will combat it with prayer and scripture and take hold of the nail-scarred hand that will never let me go.

## Day 7

Today I woke up with thankfulness on my mind, so as I made my first cup of coffee, I said my prayers. I have a new habit of posturing myself in "child's pose," which I learned from a yoga class. It not only puts me on my knees, but also folds me in half to stretch out my lower back, which I need first thing in the morning. I place my forehead directly on top of my hands and my hands are on top of my prayer list, which is on the floor in front of me. By the time I've finished praying over this list, my lower back feels much better, and then I do a bit more stretching before I'm done and start in drinking my coffee. It's been a nice way to wake up and face the day. Adding some Bible reading to this regimen is the perfect way to arm myself against Satan's attacks all day long. I wonder if he shakes with fear when he sees me limbering up at the start of the day and arming myself with the word of God and with prayer. He should—because this child of God becomes a fierce, warrior princess of the King when she's fully armed and ready!

I've always had a problem with self-discipline. Honestly, I don't always make my bed, I rarely exercise, my kitchen isn't usually clean at the end of the day, and I'm horrible at finding time to read my Bible. I *never* drink enough water, and I also hate getting up early if I'm not scheduled to work (there has to be a really good reason to get up before seven). Setting resolutions at New Year's helps for about a week, and then I tend to go back to all my old ways, which leaves me inevitably disappointed in myself. Changing my habits is a hard thing to do. I don't know if you're like me and you have a list of things you'd like to do differently, but I think the problem is that we try to make these changes in our own strength. We make our list of resolutions and begin with the statement of "I am going to do this, this, and this differently from here on out, and it's going to be life-changing." We start out very confidently with a statement like that, and for a few days we feel very proud of ourselves for demonstrating such discipline. We continue what we hope to be our new habits, and it takes next to nothing to distract us away from them. The next thing you know, we make excuses for going back to our previous ways, and then the self-loathing sets in, along with a lot of negative self-talk. We feel like utter failures. Life becomes hard again, and we aren't inspired to do any of the things on our list of resolutions. It never changed our lives. It just left us feeling terrible about ourselves.

What if, before we took on a change, we let God in on the plan? I think the reason we failed is because we tried to make a big change on our own steam, when we could have been relying on strength from God to overcome our past tendencies and natures. If we'd prayed about this thing we need to change, wouldn't the goal be more attainable? It might be. If we can really "do all things through Him who gives us strength" (Philippians 4:13), why wasn't He on the planning committee for this issue? Did we think that our issues were too petty for God to be interested in? Remember, He pays attention to even the smallest of details. Let's ensure that next time we feel the need to change a habit, we ask God for His help in achieving the goal. No matter how big or small the change is, I guarantee we'll feel stronger in the battle against our former nature if He is cheering us on.

## Day 8

Today follows an amazing and beautiful weekend in which Bryan and I rode the Harley most of Saturday. We brought all the necessary gear for temperature changes during this time of "Indian summer." Add the wind of the motorcycle to that, and the gear was much appreciated. Our destination was a burger joint out in the middle of nowhere, Illinois. After eating at the home of the "Moonburger" (which was a great burger, by the way), we found our way to the broom corn festival in Arthur, Illinois, which was nice to walk through. They had a lot of food vendors and product vendors, much like any other large fall festival. We did a bit of shopping, enjoyed a snack, and then headed back home as the sun was going down.

Sunday morning, we all attended the 9 a.m. service at our church, and the music was fabulous! Nothing gives me tingles like three-part harmony done well. Our current worship team is from Lincoln Christian University, and they're doing an internship in worship-leading at our church. Given my musical background, it takes a lot to impress me. I had a couple of tears streaming down my face during the communion meditation time. Beautiful worship to our faithful God was taking place, and it was wonderful! Bryan and I spent the afternoon doing necessary things around the house and property. He spend most of that time tilling part of the garden so that we can apply the manure, decomposed wood chips, and then solid wood chips, as we are preparing the soil for next year. The peppers, tomatoes, and Brussel sprouts are still producing, so we can't do the entire garden yet. Also, the apple tree is dropping apples into the garden, so until the good apples are picked and the tree is trimmed way down, another section of the garden waits.

I spent the afternoon making homemade pasta sauce from our tomatoes and peppers, cooking them down, and then straining and adding other ingredients for flavor. Later, I jarred and water-seal canned seven quarts of sauce. This will save on the grocery bill later if I'm not buying sauce at the store. I was really happy with the flavor, and so I think this was a good project. Very soon we will need to process apples into applesauce, apple butter, and apple pie filling. I think the apples are just about ready, and I'm sure I have more than my family needs, so we'll invite the neighbors over to pick what they want and give some things away. I tend to keep my folks and Bryan's mom stocked in applesauce all year round, along with the salsa, tomatoes, corn, and green beans that I've managed to can.

Turning to a more serious subject, today is 9/11. It brings with it very sobering thoughts of that terrorist attack upon the United States. At the same time, we have multiple hurricanes hitting us in the south and earthquakes, along with famine and other issues. We're not supposed to know when Christ is coming again, but every day I witness rage and selfishness that makes me wish He would come now and just take us with Him. America needs to return to God! Our president needs our prayers, regardless whether you like him or not. We need to long for the return of Christ the way a military wife longs for her soldier to return home from war. That's intense, I know, but we should all be getting ready and looking forward to His return.

I also have a friend from junior high school, who lost her husband a month ago due to medical negligence. They are still raising young daughters, and what happened to him was completely preventable. My friend and her daughters are grieving this terrible loss, and I'm too far away to be of any help to them, so I prayed that God would give them strength every day to keep getting up in the morning and doing the things they need to do to cope. I don't know how you deal with a loss like this in your mid-forties. I know, however, that my friend was raised in church and loves God, and I pray that they will lean on God like they never have before.

Tomorrow is also my brother's birthday, which brings me sadness. There's another chapter in this book where I describe this situation of becoming estranged. I'm sure it's hard for my parents, as they would love to be doing something for him on his birthday, too. I pray that God will fix whatever is broken. I pray that before it's too late, my brother will show up at my door and that maybe we can reconcile the past and move forward in a healthy relationship. I think that's where I have to leave things for now. Only God can fix the situation, so I trust that in His time and in His way, He will do it. I know that He is able, and He is bigger than this mess.

For now, I'm headed for my second cup of coffee and maybe some breakfast. I am working on a homemade pizza, so I can take lunch to a work friend who is home with a new baby. Holding a baby might be what I need to pull me out of this funk that I'm in at the moment, and I'm thankful for the opportunity to do something for someone else. There is always a blessing in doing things for others.

Now it is 2 p.m., and I'm home from a visit with my friend. We work for the same medical facility, and she's at home on maternity leave. I had left a photography prop at her house when we did her baby's photo shoot, and I was taking her lunch over I could visit with her, her husband, and the baby. Lunch went over well. I'd made homemade pizzas; one is still in the fridge for my family's supper, and the other small one went to my friend's house. For two hours, I was completely lost in baby bliss and totally forgot my potential financial woes and stress. My friend's husband used to work in video at some point in his life and had wanted to part with an umbrella-style light he had in storage. I'm not kidding you when I say how touched I was that he sent it home with me and said that he most likely would never need it again. At this point in my photography, I'm not quite sure how to utilize the umbrella-style light, but I'm sure with the help of the Internet, I can figure it out. What a blessing! Then, later this evening, I finally heard from a small shop downtown that I had contacted regarding selling some of my photography pieces. They stated in today's e-mail that they are "very interested" in showcasing some of my work. They needed my phone number, and I should be hearing from them soon regarding bringing in my merchandise and working with them. Today was such a good day! I'm thankful for both good friends and new connections. If the shop helps me sell some of my artwork, then I really will be supporting the family with my talents and will reach an entirely new audience. God is so good!

## Day 9

Several days have passed since I last wrote, and it's only because we've been busy with tree trimming and apple picking and processing those apples into delicious goodness. I'm incredibly thankful for the bounty of apples that came from our tree and for the skills needed to create something usable from them. Because of the height of the tree, we've picked as we trimmed and used the extendable reaching tool to get the highest ones we could. Then, as large limbs came down, we picked the rest of what was good. There's still a huge mess in the yard of limbs and rotten apples, which I imagine will take at least another week of work to deal with. There's a fair amount of firewood to be salvaged, so we will also replenish what we've used in the fire pit during family times.

I was able to speak with one of the owners of the downtown store that will feature my photography. They are very excited to work with me, and next week I'm to sign the contract and pay the October rent plus the returnable deposit. That's $120.00 I need to come up with before next Friday, but the store gets a fair amount of traffic in the fall with the holidays coming up and being right down the street from the Lincoln museum. Still, the gal I spoke with sounded very hopeful and excited that I could sell some of my work and make some money at it. I feel blessed that they are willing to take the chance of me joining them. I've ordered a few more canvas prints from the printers, so that I have a nice variety on hand. I'll mostly be featuring the blank photo cards at this point, but enlargements are always available. I think God orchestrates situations to be helpful to us, in order to bless us.

The arm really hurts today. I peeled and cut a lot of apples yesterday, so I'm paying for all that activity. Lately, any activity (including brushing my hair) requires that I ice down the arm afterward. I see the surgeon Monday, and I pray that there is a reasonable solution to fix my torn tendon and either get me back to work or that he presents some other solution. Laina has people at her work, who are interested in purchasing apple butter and applesauce from me or even salsa I made last month. Either way, I feel that God is providing for us, and I'm confident that He will continue to do so if we are faithful.

I have really enjoyed sharing the recent events of my life and how I believe God is using them to demonstrate His attention to detail. There will be moments on a daily basis in which I feel hopeful and other times I doubt. Like everyone else, I travel up and down that continuum of faith. I will continue to pray and bring God everything from my toughest issues and tears to my victories, made possible through Him. Despite the pain in my arm and the fluctuation in my bank balance, I will give Him all the praise and glory for every wonderful and good thing in my life. I will continue to look for ways to serve others and be generous with what I have because everything belongs to God, and I'm just a steward of what I've been given. My hope and prayer for you is that your faith will be renewed each day and that you will allow God to make you the very best version of yourself. Take notice of even the smallest blessings because they will overshadow any doubt that's creeping into your thoughts. Don't be afraid for the future because God's got every-thing figured out already, and you can trust that He wants only the best for His children. Read His word and be obedient. Get involved and create a network of Christian friends if you don't already have one. Every day is a gift from God. Be thankful, and joy will find you. In this, I have no doubt.

# Discussion Activities
# and Questions

**P**en Pals: Introduce yourself and share who you are and what you do. Describe your life up to the present.

**Bloom Where You're Planted:** Describe a situation in which you had to make the most of an unusual or new setting. Did things turn out differently than you imagined?

**Basket Case:** Have you ever taken part in a ministry that was just starting up? What was your role? Is there a demographic in your local are where outreach is currently needed? Discuss this opportunity with the group.

**Blessings:** Have you ever received a blessing out of the blue? What happened, share the story with the group.

**Surprise Attack:** Satan can be very crafty and can even use the ones you love to find the weakness in your armor. Have you ever experienced a blatant attack, and how did you handle it?

**Nailed It:** Read Ephesians 6:13–17 and discuss the full armor of God.

**Tea Time**: Read Revelation chapter 3. Are you hot or cold and what are some common reasons for "riding the fence"?

**Walking on the Streets of "Bling":** When have you seen something remarkable in nature that reminded you of the absolute power of God? Read Genesis chapters 1–3.

**Camouflage:** Read Ephesians chapter 2 regarding the roles of husbands and wives. Discuss practical applications. Also, have you ever been totally consumed with worries about the future? Read Romans 8:28 and discuss God's promise for times like these.

**Write Like an Apostle**: Who in your life has inspired you to be the very best version of yourself? Was it a group or individual who made the biggest impact?

**If the Dress Fits:** Why on earth would we measure ourselves by the old standard when the old is gone and the new has come? In Christ we are all new creations! Have you ever been disappointed that something from the past didn't work out for you? Read Proverbs, chapter 31. A Proverbs 31 woman isn't a size two. What impresses God is more than just skin deep. Also, read 1 Corinthians 13 about love.

**Not Just a Job:** What's your career or job, and what was your inspiration for doing that job? Also, are you helping others or providing a service somehow? Please discuss this with the group.

**Identifier:** List ten things that identify you.

**On Alert:** What types of emergencies are you prepared for? Read 1 Thessalonians 5:2. How are you getting ready for the return of Christ?

**Setting Limits:** How do you deal with loss? Read Ecclesiastes 3:1–8 about how everything has a season. How do you cope with change?

**Light Duty:** Do you encounter opportunities to talk to others about Christ? Do you work with other Christians, and do you find encouragement in that situation? Have you ever gone from being very active to "sitting on the bench" in your Christian service, and how did that make you feel?

**Tales from the Campfire:** Describe how you became a Christian. Share a memory from Christian service camp if you have one.

**Detox:** What are things in your life God is calling you to rid yourself of in order to grow closer to Him? Have you ever attended a retreat, and was it helpful?

**Forty-Something:** Share something you're thankful for.

**The Journal**: Share a story about a situation where dramatic events resulted in bring someone to Christ.

**Stranger:** No family is perfect or always gets along. If you feel comfortable, please share a family situation that you trust God to handle.

**Fearless:** Sometimes the struggles in life feel more like walking the tightrope. Share an event or situation God brought you through or gave you the courage to face.

**Ella:** Who in your life has made the biggest impact for the sake of Christ? If they have passed away, what kind of legacy did they leave?

**The Advocate:** How has God used a difficult situation to bring about a blessing?

**The Art of Letting Go:** what stage of parenting are you in, and how are you coping?

**The Grace of Exhortation:** What is your spiritual gift?

**It'll All Come out in the Wash:** The drama in life can be exhausting! How messy is your life right now? Make a list of your concerns and pass it to the person on your left. Pray over the new list in front of you.

**Journal of faith:** If you don't already, start keeping a journal and take note of even the smallest blessings. You'll be surprised at God's attention to detail.

# About the Author

Tabitha Sneeden resides in Buffalo, Illinois, with her husband Bryan of twenty-three years and their children Laina (twenty) and Brandon (seventeen). Prior to this, the family was military, serving at bases in Little Rock, Arkansas; Fairbanks, Alaska; and Grand Forks, North Dakota, during Bryan's twenty-two years in the Air Force. Tabitha earned her Bachelor of Science in Nursing degree in 1994 from MacMurray College, in Jacksonville, Illinois, and currently works as a registered nurse in Springfield, Illinois.

CPSIA information can be obtained
at www.ICGtesting.com
Printed in the USA
LVHW06s1936190318
570340LV00010B/105/P